KEY STAGE TWO
SCOTTISH LEVELS C-E

RELIGIOUS EDUCATION

BILL GENT AND LYNN GENT

Published by Scholastic Ltd,
Villiers House,
Clarendon Avenue,
Leamington Spa,
Warwickshire CV32 5PR
Text © Bill Gent and Lynn Gent
© 1997 Scholastic Ltd
567890   90123456

AUTHORS
BILL GENT AND LYNN GENT

EDITOR
CLARE GALLAHER

ASSISTANT EDITOR
KATE PEARCE

SERIES DESIGNER
LYNNE JOESBURY

DESIGNER
CLARE BREWER

ILLUSTRATIONS
MAGGIE DOWNER AND ANNABEL SPENCELEY

COVER ILLUSTRATION
JONATHAN BENTLEY
BASED ON A CONCEPT USED BY THE LONDON BOROUGH OF REDBRIDGE FOR
ITS 1995 AGREED SYLLABUS FOR RELIGIOUS EDUCATION

INFORMATION TECHNOLOGY CONSULTANT
MARTIN BLOWS

SCOTTISH 5–14 LINKS
MARGARET SCOTT AND SUSAN GOW

Designed using Aldus Pagemaker

British Library Cataloguing-in-Publication Data
A catalogue record for this book is available from the
British Library.

ISBN 0-590-53411-4

Contents

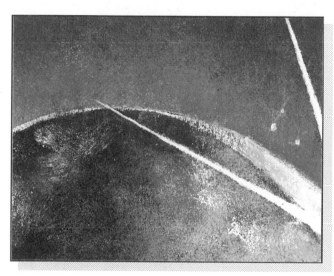

RELIGIOUS
EDUCATION

ACKNOWLEDGEMENTS

The publishers gratefully acknowledge permission to reproduce the following copyright material:

Maurice Lynch for the use of 'The Story of Kisagotami' from *RE Today* © Maurice Lynch.

The authors would like to thank Samuel Chaplain (ex-Jewish member, Redbridge SACRE), Indriyesha Das (ISKON Educational), Ngaire Moorhouse (The Clear Vision Trust), Gurinder Singh Sacha (ex-Sikh member, Redbridge SACRE), Canon Trevor Shannon (Shap Working Party).

Introduction

Scholastic Curriculum Bank is a series for all primary teachers, providing an essential planning tool for devising comprehensive schemes of work as well as an easily accessible and varied bank of practical, classroom-tested activities with photocopiable resources.

Designed to help planning for and implementation of progression, differentiation and assessment, *Scholastic Curriculum Bank RE* offers a structured range of stimulating activities with clearly stated learning objectives that should be compatible with locally agreed syllabuses for religious education, and detailed lesson plans that allow busy teachers to put the ideas into practice with the minimum amount of preparation time. The photocopiable sheets that accompany many of the activities provide ways of integrating purposeful application of knowledge and skills, differentiation, assessment and record-keeping.

Opportunities for formative assessment are highlighted where appropriate within the activities. Ways of using information technology for different purposes and within different contexts, as a tool for communicating and handling information and as a method for investigating, are integrated into the activities where appropriate and more explicit guidance is provided at the end of the book.

The series covers all the primary curriculum subjects with separate books for Key Stages 1 and 2 or Scottish Levels A–B and C–E. It can be used as a flexible resource with any scheme, to fulfil National Curriculum and Scottish 5–14 requirements and to provide children with a variety of different learning experiences that will lead to effective acquisition of skills and knowledge.

SCHOLASTIC CURRICULUM BANK RELIGIOUS EDUCATION

The *Scholastic Curriculum Bank Religious Education* books provide structured support for teachers when planning the primary religious education curriculum in the context of their locally agreed syllabus. They enable pupils to develop knowledge, understanding skills and attitudes appropriate to religious education.

Each book covers one key stage. Each book is divided into seven sections, each section covering an important aspect of religion and human experience.

Bank of activities

This book provides a bank of activities that can be used in many different ways: to supplement a scheme of work derived from the locally agreed syllabus; to add breadth and variety to an existing scheme; and to supplement a particular topic. The activities are designed to address a number of key human experiences which raise questions about belief and value, while at the same time giving children increasing familiarity with material drawn mainly from Christianity but also from the other principal religions represented in Great Britain.

Lesson plans

Detailed lesson plans, under clear headings, are given for each activity and provide material for immediate implementation in the classroom. The structure for each activity is as follows.

Activity title box

The information contained in the box at the beginning of each activity outlines the following key aspects:

▲ *Activity title and learning objective.* The activity title is given in the form of a question which relates to the learning focus of the activity and can easily be referenced to locally agreed syllabuses and Scottish 5–14 requirements by using the overview grids on pages 9 to 12. For each activity, a clearly stated learning objective or objectives is given in bold italics and will aid planning for progression.

▲ *Examples of concepts.* For each activity two important underlying concepts are given.

▲ *Class organisation/Likely duration.* Icons ✝✝ and 🕐 signpost the suggested group sizes for each activity and the approximate amount of time required to complete it.

Key background information

The information in this section provides guidance about how the activity contributes to religious education and also provides a context for religious material so that the teacher might feel confident in referring to it.

Preparation

Advice is given for those occasions where it is necessary for the teacher to prepare materials, or to set up a display or activity ahead of time.

Resources needed

All of the materials needed to carry out the activity are listed, so that the pupils or the teacher can gather them together easily before the beginning of the teaching session. There is also a main resource list, 'Useful books and resources', which is on pages 109 to 110.

What to do

Easy-to-follow, step-by-step instructions are given for carrying out the activity, including (where appropriate) suggested questions for the teacher to ask the pupils in order to help instigate discussion, stimulate exploration and encourage reflection.

Suggestion(s) for extension/ support

Ideas are given for ways of providing easy differentiation where activities lend themselves to this purpose. Suggestions are provided as to how each activity can be modified for the less able) or extended for the more able.

Assessment opportunities

Where appropriate, opportunities for ongoing teacher assessment of the children's work during or after a specific activity are highlighted. The assessment of knowledge, understanding and skills can be carried out in religious education. The assessment of attitudes, however, is often inappropriate.

Opportunities for IT

Where opportunities for IT present themselves these are briefly outlined with reference to suitable types of program. The chart on page 159 presents specific areas of IT covered in the activities, together with more detailed support on how to apply particular types of program. Selected lesson plans

serve as models for other activities by providing more comprehensive guidance on the application of IT, and these are indicated by the bold page numbers on the grid and the 💻 icon at the start of an activity.

Display/assembly ideas

Where relevant, display ideas are incorporated into activity plans. In those cases where the material lends itself to inclusion in an assembly or act of collective worship, ideas about how this might be done are given and include suggestions for themes and a closing thought or reflection.

Reference to photocopiable sheets

Where activities include photocopiable activity sheets, small reproductions of these are included in the lesson plans together with notes on how they should be used.

Assessment

Each activity presents advice on what the teacher should look out for during the course of the activity. The notes made while observing the children can contribute to a descriptive profile of the child's performance, compiled and refined throughout the school year, which might also be supported by annotated samples of the work that the child produces. Assessment is integrated into everyday performance. The activities have been designed so that they can be used as individual tasks to provide the teacher with ongoing evaluation of children's progress (formative assessment). Alternatively, certain activities can be used for summative assessment at the end of Key Stage 2. Those activities most appropriate for summative assessment are highlighted by the 📝 icon.

Photocopiable activity sheets

Many of the activities are accompanied by photocopiable activity sheets. For some activities, there will be more than one version in order to provide differentiation by task. Some sheets are more open-ended, to provide differentiation by outcome. Other sheets provide simplified versions of stories from religious and other traditions which teachers may otherwise find difficult to obtain. The photocopiable activity sheets provide purposeful activities that are ideal for assessment and can be kept as records in pupils' portfolios of work.

Cross-curricular links

Cross-curricular links are identified on a simple grid which cross-references the particular areas of study in RE to the programmes of study for other subjects in the curriculum, and where appropriate provides suggestions for activities.

Glossary

To assist teachers in their understanding of key terms from Christianity and the other principal religions, a short glossary is provided on pages 107 to 109.

RELIGIOUS EDUCATION WITHIN THE CURRICULUM

Religious education and the law

Unless partially or wholly withdrawn by parents, all registered pupils (but not including pupils in nursery classes or schools) are required to have religious education as part of their curriculum. The 1988 Education Reform Act used the term 'basic curriculum' to describe the National Curriculum and religious education together.

Locally agreed syllabuses

One of the reasons why religious education was not included in the National Curriculum was because the religious education curriculum is a matter for each local education authority to decide. The principles upon which religious education stands, and the requirements which most schools must follow (apart from voluntary aided schools, that is) are made clear in the locally agreed syllabus for religious education. The local body which brings together the material for an agreed syllabus is called an Agreed Syllabus Conference. The 1988 Education Reform Act stipulated that all locally agreed syllabuses published thereafter should 'reflect the fact that the religious traditions in Great Britain are in the main Christian whilst taking account of the teaching and practices of the other principal religions represented in Great Britain'.

National guidelines in Scotland

In Scotland the Scottish Office Education Department has issued national guidelines for the 5–14 age group for the five curricular areas, one of which is Religious and Moral Education (RME). The RME programme includes aspects of Personal and Social Development (PSD) which explore moral values and relationships. PSD is not a curricular area, but it permeates all studies across the curriculum. National guidelines for PSD have been produced to ensure systematic planning. The RME guidelines are structured under the headings 'Christianity', 'Other world religions' and 'Personal search'.

The national model material

To assist Agreed Syllabus Conferences in following the requirements of the 1988 Act, the Schools Curriculum and Assessment Authority (SCAA) published a series of booklets in 1994. One contained advice from working parties representing Christianity and the other principal religious traditions (Buddhism, Hinduism, Islam, Judaism and Sikhism). Another contained a glossary of terms for each religion. Further booklets suggested two attainment targets for religious education – 'learning about religion' and 'learning from religion' – and outlined how religious content might be structured in an agreed syllabus so as to further educational aims. These booklets have been consulted in the production of *Scholastic Curriculum Bank Religious Education*.

Religious education and collective worship

It is important that, in planning and thinking, religious education and collective worship are seen as distinct and separate aspects of school life. The legal requirements for each are different though, as with religious education, parents have the right to withdraw their children from daily collective worship (though not, technically speaking, from assembly). Most local education authorities have produced guidance on collective worship separate to that on religious education. Nevertheless, there can be a fruitful overlap between religious education and collective worship. For this reason, some of the activities in this book suggest ways in which material and insights from work in religious education might be used to support meaningful acts of collective worship.

RELIGIOUS EDUCATION AT KEY STAGE 2

At all key stages, there are two dimensions to religious education, though how particular agreed syllabuses express this might differ. One dimension involves the exploration of religion in its many forms and contexts. The other involves children investigating and reflecting upon their own lifestyles and experiences. The two dimensions are inextricably linked, however, and activities in religious education often involve both at one and the same time. In looking at 'pilgrimage' in religion, for example, teachers will usually encourage children to think about special journeys that they themselves have made. It was for this reason that the national model syllabuses (see above) spoke of two attainment targets: 'learning about religion' and 'learning from religion'.

The respective emphasis given to each of the two dimensions of religious education will differ as pupils progress through each key stage. At Key Stage 3 there is often a heavy emphasis on learning about religions. At Key Stage 1, there is usually a heavy emphasis on children reflecting on their own experiences and the many things and people which stand out as 'special'. While this emphasis continues during Key Stage 2, it is usual for pupils also to be introduced to explicitly religious material drawn from Christianity and several other principal religions. Religious education has often been described as that part of the curriculum which, *par excellence*, is concerned with worth and value. It is its role in encouraging children to reflect on their own experiences that also gives it its central place in the spiritual development of children, though of course this responsibility is not exclusive to religious education.

Because a number of the activities at Key Stage 2 involve looking at and reflecting on special things – objects, people, places and events – it will be important for the teacher to think about context and atmosphere. Some teachers use a 'stilling exercise' to prepare for some work in religious education. Others will place an artefact into a 'feely' bag, made of material such as velvet, to emphasise its worth.

Most schools now have their own collections of religious artefacts, and teachers are becoming increasingly competent in using them. There is no one 'correct' way of using an artefact, of course, though a three-fold process has often been identified: the 'puzzling' stage (in which the artefact is investigated and clues to its meaning and use sought), the 'supplementing' stage (in which additional information is supplied) and the 'personalising' stage (in which links with the lives of the children are explored).

Note on dating: The abbreviations used after some dates in this book follow the convention which is now universally used in literature dealing with a number of religions. Instead of the older BC, the abbreviation BCE (before the common era) is used and instead of AD, the abbreviation CE (common era) is used.

Overview grid

Learning objective	RE focus	Content	Type of activity	Page
Living with ourselves				
To identify a person who is admired because of his or her qualities. To understand some of the reasons why Sikhs admire Guru Nanak.	Year 3/4; P4/5 *Personal Search, Other World Religions – Moral values: Level B.* Sikhism	Looking at a Sikh artefact, listening to a Sikh story, identifying people who are most admired.	Whole class looking at artefact, followed by small-group work. Individual completion of photocopiable sheet.	14
To reflect on personal experiences which can give rise to pride and shame. To consider the feelings and experiences of others.	Year 3/4; P4/5 *Personal Search – Moral values: Level C* Human experience	Role-playing situations which give rise to feelings of pride and shame. Writing accounts of personal experiences.	Group role-play followed by whole class listening to story, ending with individual work.	15
To understand that the possession of wealth raises a number of deep issues. To know and understand a story from the Sikh tradition.	Year 3/4; P4/5 *Personal Search, Other World Religions – Moral values: Level C* Sikhism	Identifying the good and bad aspects of being wealthy. Listening to and discussing a Sikh story about wealth.	Paired discussion followed by whole class and ending with paired work.	17
To identify important personal beliefs or convictions. To understand that some people have such strong beliefs and convictions that they are willing to die for them.	Year 5/6; P5/7 *Personal Search, Other World Religions – Beliefs: Level C* Islam	Identifying own convictions before listening to a Muslim story. Writing a diary extract or imaginary situation.	Individual completion of photocopiable sheet. Paired discussion, whole class listening to story, individual writing.	19
To encourage an interest in the role and range of beliefs and ideas. To understand that 'God' means different things to different people.	Year 5/6; P6/7 *Christianity, Other World Religions – Beliefs: Level C/D* Human experience	Looking at what children think of when they hear the word 'God'. Carrying out a survey with other classes.	Whole-class observation and discussion followed by group work, then returning to whole class.	20
To understand that the truth is sometimes hard to accept. To know that compassion is a central Buddhist teaching.	Year 5/6; P6/7 *Personal Search, Other World Religions – Moral values: Level C* Buddhism	Listening to a Buddhist story about wisdom and compassion. Responding to questions about it.	Whole-class discussion, then small-group work returning to whole class.	21
To understand that being tempted is a significant human experience. To know about an episode in the life of Jesus.	Year 5/6; P6/7 *Christianity, Personal Search – Moral values: Level C/D* Christianity	Groups discussing examples of being tempted, hearing an account of the temptations of Jesus, writing their own temptation story.	Groups working on photocopiable sheet. Whole-class discussion, ending with individual work.	23
Living with others				
To know one of Jesus' parables. To understand that love of others is a central Christian teaching.	Year 3/4; P4/5 *Christianity – Stories: Level B* Christianity	Discussing and dramatising the parable of the Good Samaritan; understanding its importance for Christians.	Whole class listening to story. Group work, returning to whole class and ending with group work.	26
To understand that memories can be evoked by physical objects. To develop the capacity to reflect on relationships and past experiences.	Year 3/4; P4/5 *Personal Search – Relationships and moral values: Level C* Human experience	Looking at how items made of fabric can evoke family memories, hearing a story and then individually creating a 'patchwork quilt'.	Whole class looking at items, followed by individual work.	28
To develop the capacity to reflect on relationships. To develop the ability to empathise with others.	Year 3/4; P4/5 *As above: Level C* Human experience	Thinking about the relationship between sisters and brothers, listening to a story, writing about incidents from two points of view.	Group work followed by whole class contributing. Paired completion of photocopiable sheet.	29
To know a story from the Hindu tradition. To identify a range of feelings associated with naughtiness.	Year 3/4; P4/5 *As above: Level D* Hinduism	Recollecting occasions when children have been naughty, listening to and discussing a Hindu story, writing own story.	Small groups followed by whole class listening to story, then individual writing.	31
To interpret the teaching of a story from a religious tradition. To identify some of the consequences of different forms of behaviour towards others.	Year 5/6; P6/7 *As above: Level D* Sikhism	Identifying the teaching behind a Sikh story, thinking about the consequences resulting from responding to a school situation.	Paired completion of photocopiable sheet. Whole class contributing, then return to paired work finishing with whole class.	32

9

RELIGIOUS EDUCATION

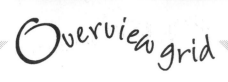
Learning objective	RE focus	Content	Type of activity	Page
To understand that different people have different lifestyles. To develop the attitudes of fairness and respect.	Year 5/6; P6/7 *Personal Search – Relationships and moral values: Level D* Human experience	Reflecting on different lifestyles, discussing what makes your own house a home, then writing an account.	Whole class listening to story, paired discussion and ending with individual work.	34
To deepen an understanding of how relationships develop. To develop the ability to see the world through the eyes of others, and to see issues from their point of view.	Year 5/6; P6/7 *As above: Level D* Human experience	Using the three characters in a story as a stimulus, exploring what happens when we want to keep people to ourselves.	Whole class listening to story, group discussion, trios and ending with individual writing.	35
Living in the world				
To understand that people have always asked questions about how the world began. To form a judgement about what should or should not be included in a 'perfect' new world.	Year 3/4; P4/5 *Personal Search – The natural world: Level C* Human experience	Considering how the world began, looking at responses, deciding what would and would not be included in a newly created world.	Group work followed by whole class and ending with paired work.	38
To identify personal feelings towards Earth as a planet. To understand that there are a variety of responses to the use or abuse of the planet.	Year 3/4; P4/5 *As above: Level C* Human experience	Responding to a picture of the Earth, discussing the meaning of a story and identifying the viewpoints of the characters.	Whole class looking at a picture; individual responses.	39
To know that some people care for living things for religious reasons. To encourage an attitude of respect for living things.	Year 3/4; P4/5 *As above: Level C* Hinduism	Responding to an incident when a ladybird is stamped on, talking about the place of the cow in Hinduism and planning a 'Caring for Living Things Week'.	Group discussion followed by whole class contributing, returning to group work.	41
To identify key beliefs and ideas within a piece of Christian devotional writing. To identify and express some of their own ideas and beliefs about harvest.	Year 3/4; P4/5 *As above: Level C* Christianity	Investigating a Christian harvest hymn in order to identify its beliefs and ideas; writing own verse about harvest.	Whole class then group work, returning to whole class and ending with individual writing.	43
To know a story from the Judaeo-Christian tradition. To understand that story can convey truths about human nature.	Year 5/6; P6/7 *As above: Level D* Judaism; Christianity	Looking at the story of Adam and Eve as a way of discussing the human condition; devising a role-play to express this.	Whole class followed by small group work, returning to class discussion, then small group role-play.	44
To know a key story connected with the life of the Buddha. To identify aspects of the world that give rise to ultimate questions.	Year 5/6; P6/7 *Personal Search – Ultimate questions: Level D* Buddhism	Thinking about what sights might challenge the view that life is all about pleasure, listening to a story about the Buddha and mounting a class display.	Group completion of photocopiable sheet, followed by whole class, ending with group work.	46
To identify some of the ways in which trees are important to themselves and others. To understand how trees can become a focus of story and ritual.	Year 5/6; P6/7 *Personal Search – The natural world: Level C* Human experience	Exploring feelings about trees. Learning about trees in religions, thinking about how important times could focus on a special tree.	Whole-class discussion, large groups, whole class. Then whole class followed by individual work.	48
Following guidance				
To know a story associated with a number of major religious traditions. To identify times in your own life when you have avoided following instructions.	Year 3/4; P4/5 *Christianity, Other World Religions – Moral values and attitudes: Level B/C* Judaism; Christianity; Islam	Listening to the first part of the Jonah story, working on sections of it, identifying times when the children have tried to avoid following instructions.	Whole class listening to story, followed by small groups, returning to whole class then individual work.	52
To understand the role of key words in binding a group together. To understand the importance of the Shema for Jews.	Year 3/4; P4/5 *Other World Religions – Sacred places, worship and symbols: Level D* Judaism	Agreeing a key statement and ways in which it could be used, looking at a mezuzah case, designing a special container for the key statement.	Group completion of photocopiable sheet, followed by whole-class observation and ending with paired or individual work.	54
To know a story concerning the life of Jesus. To understand that many Christians would follow Jesus' example in reacting to situations of inappropriate behaviour or injustice.	Year 3/4; P4/5 *Christianity – Stories: Level B* Christianity	Exploring experiences of anger, looking at a story in which Jesus showed anger, deciding what might make a Christian follow Jesus' example.	Whole-class discussion and listening to story, followed by paired work.	56

RELIGIOUS
EDUCATION

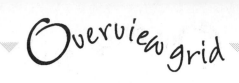

Learning objective	RE focus	Content	Type of activity	Page
To know that Sikhs consult their holy book in choosing a child's name. To encourage an interest in naming customs and the origin of names.	Year 3/4; P4/5 *Other World Religions – Ceremonies and customs: Level C* Sikhism	Discussing how first names are chosen, learning about the Sikh naming tradition, decorating names.	Whole-class discussion followed by individual work.	57
To understand some of the ways in which books of guidance offer support. To know that the Bible offers guidance to Christians.	Year 5/6; P6/7 *Christianity – Sacred writings: Level C* Christianity	Thinking about how a booklet could help a new child, describing the Bible as a book for guidance for Christians, identifying a personal book of guidance.	Small group work, whole-class discussion and then individual writing.	59
To know what the Five Pillars of Islam are. To understand how rules and duties can guide a community.	Year 5/6; P6/7 *Other World Religions – Sacred writings: Level C* Islam	Identifying things which could unite two amalgamating schools, learning about each of the Five Pillars.	Group work, whole-class discussion, individual completion of photocopiable sheet.	61
To understand the role of promises in human experience. To understand how the Five Precepts might affect the life of a Buddhist.	Year 5/6; P6/7 *As above: Level C* Buddhism	Discussing the place of promises in human experience, detecting how the Five Precepts might affect a Buddhist.	Whole-class discussion, individual completion of photocopiable sheet, returning to whole class.	63

Encountering special times

Learning objective	RE focus	Content	Type of activity	Page
To know the key events associated with Holy Week. To know some of the ways in which Christians today remember and relive these events.	Year 3/4; P4/5 *Christianity – Celebrations, festivals, ceremonies and customs: Level B* Christianity	Finding out what the children already know about Easter, learning about the key days in Holy Week, producing a summary in words and pictures.	Group work followed by whole class listening and ending with individual completion of photocopiable sheet.	66
To understand why light is used as a symbol at Christmas. To know how Christians might interpret the symbolism of a Christingle.	Year 3/4; P4/5 *As above: Level C* Christianity	Thinking of ways in which light is used at Christmas, looking at the symbolism of a Christingle, recording understanding.	Individual writing followed by whole-class work, individual completion of photocopiable sheet.	68
To compare and contrast material from different sources. To consider and raise questions about the different Christian accounts of what happened on the first Easter Sunday morning.	Year 5/6; P6/7 *As above: Level C* Christianity	Recounting the events of Holy Week, summarising the Gospel accounts of Easter Sunday morning, discussing similarities and differences.	Whole-class listening followed by small groups, ending with whole-class discussion.	70
To understand that the traditional Christmas story derives from several sources. To compare and contrast material from different sources.	Year 5/6; P6/7 *As above: Level C* Christianity	Exploring the Christmas story, learning about the two biblical sources, comparing and contrasting these sources.	Paired work, whole-class listening, paired completion of photocopiable sheet.	73
To understand the importance of Bar Mitzvah and Bat Mitzvah within the Jewish community. To know what several Jewish artefacts are and how they relate to Bar Mitzvah and Bat Mitzvah.	Year 5/6; P6/7 *Other World Religions – Celebrations, festivals, ceremonies and customs: Level C* Judaism	Examining several artefacts, learning about Bar and Bat Mitzvah, writing an account including reference to Jewish artefacts.	Whole class looking at and discussing artefact, individual completion of photocopiable sheet.	75
To reflect on aspects of experience related to seeking forgiveness. To understand the significance of Rosh Hashanah and Yom Kippur for Jews.	Year 5/6; P6/7 *As above: Level C* Judaism	Thinking about times involving the wish for forgiveness, learning about what Jews do at these two festivals.	Friendship pairs followed by class discussion, individual completion of photocopiable sheet.	77

Encountering special places

Learning objective	RE focus	Content	Type of activity	Page
To encourage reflection on the range of feelings associated with a place where a person has been happy. To express feelings using an appropriate medium.	Year 3/4; P4/5 *Other World Religions – Sacred places, worship and symbols: Level B* Human experience	Exploring the feelings described in a story, talking about places where we remember being happy, choosing a medium to express them.	Whole class listening to story, small-group discussion and then individual work.	80
To know some of the key features of a church building. To understand that what Christians believe to be important is reflected in a church building.	Year 3/4; P4/5 *Christianity – Sacred places, worship and symbols: Level B/C* Christianity	Visiting a church building, noting the features and meeting a church member, making links between important things for Christians and the building.	Class visit to church, paired completion of photocopiable sheet.	81

RELIGIOUS EDUCATION

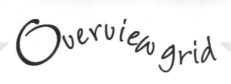

Learning objective	RE focus	Content	Type of activity	Page
To understand what makes the synagogue a special place for Jews. To know the significance of the ark within the synagogue.	Year 3/4; P4/5 *Other World Religions – Sacred places, worship and symbols: Level D* Judaism	Talking about where special objects are kept, learning about what the ark is used for in a synagogue, consolidating what has been learned.	Whole class looking at a special object, individual completion of photocopiable sheet.	83
To know the key features associated with a mosque. To know the purpose of these key features.	Year 3/4; P4/5 *As above: Level D* Islam	Learning about what a qiblah compass is used for, looking at the main features of a mosque.	Whole class looking at artefact and ground-plan, individual completion of photocopiable sheet.	85
To understand the place of the Ka'bah in Muslim thoughts and feelings. To know the place of the Ka'bah in Muslim pilgrimage.	Year 5/6; P6/7 *As above: Level B/C* Islam	Learning about the importance of the Ka'bah for Muslims, discussing the feelings of a pilgrim, writing an account.	Whole class looking at picture or video extract, paired work, individual completion of photocopiable sheet.	88
To know what physical features of a gurdwara are related to the Sikh holy book. To acquire general information about a Sikh gurdwara.	Year 5/6; P6/7 *As above: Level C* Sikhism	Designing a room to house a special book, learning about the room in which the Sikh holy book is kept, writing an imaginary architect's report.	Group work, class discussion, then individual work.	89
To know some of the features and activities associated with a mandir (temple). To understand that visiting a place of worship raises a variety of issues.	Year 5/6; P6/7 *As above: Level C* Hinduism	Reading an imaginary account of a first visit to a Hindu temple, responding to questions raised by it, discussing responses and looking at resources.	Pairs reading and completing photocopiable sheet, followed by whole class looking at artefacts.	91

Expressing what is important

Learning objective	RE focus	Content	Type of activity	Page
To understand some Christian beliefs and ideas about life and death. To know and understand some examples of Christian symbolism.	Year 3/4; P4/5 *Personal Search – The natural world: Level C* Christianity	Pre-visit briefing, visiting a graveyard to find evidence for Christian beliefs and ideas about life and death, discussing findings after the visit.	Whole-class discussion, individual work during the visit, whole class after the visit.	94
To understand why Muslims use Arabesque and calligraphy. To express beliefs, values and ideas in pictorial form.	Year 3/4; P4/5 *Other World Religions – Sacred writings: Level C* Islam	Looking at examples of Muslim calligraphy and Arabesque, learning about underlying beliefs and ideas, completing a design task for a school.	Individuals looking at photocopiable sheet, class discussion, individual or paired work.	96
To understand that Remembrance Day fulfils a variety of roles and needs. To understand that ritual and ceremony are a means by which people express feelings.	Year 3/4; P4/5 *Christianity – Ceremonies: Level D* Human experience	Thinking about what happens on Remembrance Day and why, creating school rituals which could be used to remember a serious event.	Whole-class discussion followed by group work.	98
To know the titles and meanings of a number of crosses. To design and explain the meaning of a variation of the Christian cross.	Year 5/6; P6/7 *Christianity – Symbols: Level D* Christianity	Looking at different types of cross, thinking about how shape can suggest ideas and beliefs, designing a cross.	Whole-class discussion followed by individual work.	100
To understand the link between bodily positions and inward attitudes and beliefs. To encourage respect for those who have different beliefs and customs.	Year 5/6; P6/7 *Christianity, Other World Religions – Worship: Level D* Christianity; Judaism; Islam	Thinking of bodily positions that people might adopt for prayer, looking at examples drawn from three religions, consolidating what has been learned.	Whole class followed by individual work.	102
To understand that stories convey teachings. To detect teachings within a story.	Year 5/6; P6/7 *Other World Religions – Symbols: Level D* Hinduism	Looking at a Hindu artefact, analysing a story to see what it teaches, agreeing the most important part of the story.	Whole class looking at picture or artefact, followed by paired work, returning to whole class.	103
To understand how symbolism can be an expression of feelings and experiences. To encourage the ability to see the world through the eyes of others.	Year 5/6; P6/7 *As above: Level C/D* Human experience	Listening to a story about an imaginary village, discussing the story, carrying out design and planning tasks.	Whole class listening to story and responding, followed by group work.	105

Entries given in italics relate to the Scottish 5–14 Guidelines for Religious and Moral Education.

RELIGIOUS EDUCATION

Living with ourselves

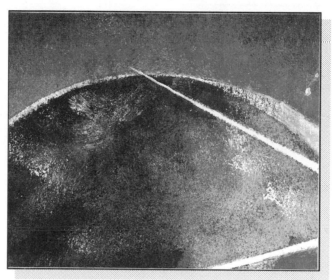

Religious education is not concerned solely with things obviously 'religious'. It is also concerned with addressing and exploring a range of experiences, particularly those which raise issues of belief and value, meaning and purpose. Many of these experiences raise what have been termed 'ultimate or final questions', such as 'Who am I? What is the meaning of relationships? What is the purpose and meaning of life? What is the difference between right and wrong?'

Thus, in this chapter, some activities give children the opportunity to explore and respond to a number of key personal experiences – feeling proud or ashamed, the sense of being tempted, and refusing to accept what you know to be true.

Other activities focus on how ideas and beliefs shape each individual. Children are given the opportunity to identify the qualities of the person they admire most, to think about what beliefs and convictions they would defend to the last, and to explore the meaning of 'being wealthy'.

Finally, it is suggested that older Key Stage 2 pupils be given the opportunity to make sense of what people associate with the word 'God'.

Most of these activities combine both dimensions of religious education: 'learning about religion' – material is drawn from the Buddhist, Christian, Muslim and Sikh traditions – and 'learning from religion'.

RELIGIOUS
EDUCATION

WHO DO I ADMIRE MOST?

To identify a person who is admired because of his or her qualities. To understand some of the reasons why Sikhs admire Guru Nanak.

Admiration. Quality.

†† *Whole class followed by small group work and then individual work.*

🕐 *Whole class 20 minutes; small group work 10 minutes; individual work 30 minutes.*

Key background information

Stories which are told about founders of religions or key religious figures are not usually told 'just' for entertainment: they carry messages about the person or persons in the story and teaching about how followers should live their lives.

Sikhs tell many stories about the founder of their religion, Guru Nanak (1469–1539). The message of many of the ones that concern his childhood, for example, is that, even as a child, Nanak was marked out as special. (In one story, for instance, Nanak sat in the shade of a tree and fell asleep. The sun moved, but miraculously the shade remained in order to protect him.)

Pictures of Guru Nanak abound and usually show him as a gentle-looking, white-bearded elderly man, wearing a turban and with a hand raised in a blessing. A halo of light usually surrounds his head. Wedding garlands are often placed around the neck of the bride and groom during the wedding ceremony at a Sikh *gurdwara* (place of worship). A portrait of one of the Sikh Gurus – there were ten in all – is sometimes placed in the heart-shaped part of the garland which hangs at the front, though not all Sikhs feel comfortable with this practice.

This activity gives children the opportunity to learn about an aspect of the Sikh religion as well as to reflect on their own values as personified in those people they themselves most admire.

Preparation

Obtain a Sikh wedding garland with a picture of Guru Nanak and place in a velvet bag. Make a copy of photocopiable page 112 and become familiar with the story of Guru Nanak. Make copies of photocopiable page 113, one for each child.

Resources needed

Sikh wedding garland; velvet bag; photocopiable pages 112 and 113; writing and drawing materials.

What to do

Gather the children together in a circle and tell them that you are going to show them something which is special for a group of people called Sikhs. Carefully take the wedding garland out of the bag, ensuring that all the children are able to see it. Ask the children questions to encourage them to look closely at the artefact.

▲ How do you know that this person is important?
▲ Do you think this person is kind or unkind?
▲ Why is this person's hand raised?
▲ Would you like to meet this person?

Tell the children that the artefact is called a wedding garland because it is used in Sikh weddings. The picture in the wedding garland is of Guru Nanak who Sikhs greatly admire began he founded their religion about 500 years ago. Sikhs call him a *Guru*, which means teacher, because he taught them about God and how to live their lives. Explain to the children that Sikhs love to tell stories about Guru Nanak which reveal his qualities. They are going to hear a story about something that Nanak did when he was a young man. Read the story on photocopiable page 112.

Ask the children which qualities of Guru Nanak's they think are demonstrated in the story.

Divide the children into small groups and ask them to talk about the people whom they admire and what it is about them that they most respect. Visit each group in turn and encourage all the children to take part in the discussion.

When everyone has had the opportunity to talk about the person they admire most, give each child a copy of photocopiable page 113 and ask them to complete it.

RELIGIOUS EDUCATION

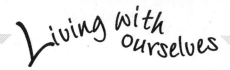

Suggestion(s) for extension

Encourage children to use the school library to find other stories which Sikhs tell about Guru Nanak. They should read these stories and make a list of Guru Nanak's qualities which they find in them.

Suggestion(s) for support

Instead of completing photocopiable page 113, give children a separate sheet of paper. Ask them to draw a picture of the person they admire most and underneath their drawing to complete the starter sentences 'The name of my person is...' and ' I admire this person because...'

Assessment opportunities

Photocopiable page 113, and the sheet which the children complete in the support activity, will provide evidence of the extent to which they have been able to identify a person whom they admire. The discussion following the reading of the story about Guru Nanak will provide general evidence as to whether the children have understood some of the reasons why Sikhs admire Guru Nanak.

Opportunities for IT

Allow the children to use an encyclopaedia CD-ROM to find further information on the life of Guru Nanak. Alternatively, they could use a specific religious resource such as the Nelson *Media Aspects of Religion* CD-ROM.

Display ideas

Divide a display board into halves vertically. Give one half the title 'Guru Nanak is admired by Sikhs' and mount a copy of the story, together with the qualities that the children detected in it. The Sikh wedding garland and the lists of qualities found in other stories could also be displayed. Give the other half of the board the title 'These are people that we admire' and mount a selection of the completed photocopiable sheets.

Reference to photocopiable sheets

Photocopiable page 112 contains a copy of the story of Guru Nanak which should be told to the children during the activity. Photocopiable page 113 is designed to help children identify the person that they admire most and to focus on his or her qualities.

WHEN DO I FEEL PROUD OR ASHAMED OF MYSELF?

To reflect on personal experiences which can give rise to pride and shame. To consider the feelings and experiences of others.

Identity. Feelings.

†† *Groups followed by whole class and then individual work.*

🕘 *Group work 20 minutes; whole class 15 minutes; individual 25 minutes.*

Key background information

Though this activity does not include anything explicitly 'religious', it does involve children in using processes and developing skills which are central to religious education, notably *reflection* and *empathy*. The former, according to the SCAA model syllabuses (see Introduction, page 8), includes the ability to reflect on feelings, relationships and experience, whereas empathy includes the ability to consider the thoughts, feelings, experiences, attitudes, beliefs and values of others.

Preparation

Collect a variety of local newspapers.

Resources needed

Writing materials. For the extension activity – local newspapers.

What to do

Divide the children into groups of about six. Give the groups two situations to discuss and then tell them to choose one of the situations overleaf to role-play.

▲ An eight-year-old child notices several bottles of milk left on an elderly neighbour's doorstep. The child knows that the neighbour is at home and has not been well recently, so decides to find out whether help is needed. This results in the discovery that the neighbour has been injured falling down the stairs. The neighbour is taken to hospital where a reporter from a local newspaper hears what has happened and writes an article about the part played by the child.

▲ Year 4 is going on a visit to a local museum which will cost each child five pounds. Today is the last opportunity for children to bring in their money. One child drops her five-pound note in the playground where it is found by a child from a different year group. The child who finds the money puts it in her pocket and doesn't tell anyone. The child who lost the five-pound note thinks that she will not be able to go on the trip. During the morning, the five-pound note falls out of the pocket of the child who found the money. She is sent to the headteacher, who finds out what happened.

Ask the children to use body language, including facial expression, during their role-plays. Set a time limit for their completion. While the groups are working, listen to and observe each group.

Ask several groups in turn to show one of the situations to the whole class before choosing other groups to show their interpretation of the other situation.

Discuss the two situations, focusing particularly on the feelings of the two children once their actions have become public. Introduce into the discussion the two emotional reactions of 'pride' and 'shame'. Ask the question: 'Are we always proud of everything that we do?' Encourage volunteers to share their own experiences of times when they have felt proud and times when they have felt ashamed.

To complete the activity, ask the children to each write a 'newspaper article' based around an incident when they have either felt proud or ashamed of something that they have done.

Suggestion(s) for extension
In addition to their own newspaper article, children could look through local newspapers to find articles reporting situations which have resulted in the feelings of pride and shame.

Suggestion(s) for support
Children who find the final written task difficult could be asked to draw a series of pictures, using speech bubbles to depict either a shameful or a proud incident.

Opportunities for IT
Let the children use a newspaper package or a desktop publishing package to write their newspaper article about a time when they felt ashamed or proud of something. A master page layout could be set up beforehand or children could create their own. The children could also scan in photographs of themselves to illustrate the article.

Assembly ideas
As part of an assembly focusing on a theme such as 'Making choices' or 'In the news', ask a child to begin by making a short statement about how life presents situations in which we may feel pride or shame. A number of 'articles' describing such situations could then be read out, some written by the children themselves and others taken from local newspapers. Two groups of children can then each show one of the class role-plays. You may like to end the assembly with a reflection such as, 'And now, in a moment of quiet, let us think about those many times in life when we have to make a choice. Let us hope that the choices that we do make will give us the feeling of pride and not of shame.'

WILL BEING RICH MAKE ME A GOOD PERSON?

To understand that the possession of wealth raises a number of deep issues. To know and understand a story from the Sikh tradition.

Wealth. Goodness.

Pairs followed by whole class and then paired work.
Pairs 10 minutes; whole class 30 minutes; paired work 30 minutes.

Key background information

It is because the desire for wealth and material possessions can so easily dominate people's lives – becoming, as it were, an object of 'worship' – that teaching about wealth and possessions is found in all religious traditions. The saying of Jesus that 'It is harder for a rich man to enter the kingdom of heaven than for a camel to pass through the eye of a needle' (Luke's Gospel, chapter 18, verse 25) is a familiar one.

The story chosen for this activity is from the Sikh tradition. In its more 'authentic' Sikh version, it is pooree (a small, fried pancake) that represents the rich person's food and roti (simple, coarse bread, pronounced 'rote-ee') the poor person's. Milk, coming as it does from the cow, which is sacred in India, represents purity in its Indian context.

Because of the honour in which they hold their ten Gurus, some Sikhs might object to children playing the part of a Guru in a play. If, therefore, the story is going to be acted, it might be wise to seek the opinion of any Sikh parents in the school.

Preparation

Make a copy of photocopiable page 114 and become familiar with the story. Make copies for the children if you intend to give it to them when they are completing their tasks.

Resources needed

Photocopiable page 114; chalkboard/flip chart; writing and drawing materials.

What to do

Ask the children to work in pairs and to make lists of good things and bad things about being rich. Visit the pairs while they are working, asking the children with very good ideas to read them out to the rest of the class. (This will be particularly helpful for adding to the list of bad things.)

After a specified time, bring the class together and make a main list on the board (a child could do the scribing). Talk briefly abut each suggestion. Tell the children that there are stories in all the religions of the world which seek to show what happens to people when they become wealthy or spend all their time trying to gain wealth. Next, explain that they are going to hear a story which Sikhs tell about a man called Guru Nanak, who began their religion about 500 years ago. Read or tell the story on photocopiable page 114.

Ask questions about the story to encourage the children to search out the messages within it.

▲ Why did Nanak choose to go to Lalo's house?

▲ Why did Malik Bhago ask Guru Nanak to his house?

▲ What was Guru Nanak trying to show when he squeezed the cake and bread?

▲ Do you think that Malik Bhago was happier before or after Guru Nanak's visit?

Working in their pairs, ask the children to choose one of the following tasks. They can:

▲ write the story of Malik Bhago and Lalo in the form of a play;

▲ write a straightforward account of the story;

▲ tell the story using a series of pictures with speech bubbles and/or running commentary.

Suggestion(s) for extension

Children, imagining that they have been left a large amount of money by a relative, could write an account of what happens to them, bringing out both good and bad points.

Suggestion(s) for support

Make sure that the less confident children work with a partner who can offer them support.

Assessment opportunities

A number of elements in this activity will provide evidence of the extent to which the children understand the implications of wealth. These include the positive and negative aspects

of wealth identified by pairs, and the imaginary accounts written by those children carrying out the extension activity. The discussion after you have told the story, and the results of the written tasks, will indicate the extent to which the meanings underlying the story have been grasped.

Opportunities for IT

Those children who choose to write the story of Malik Bhago and Lalo in the form of a play could use a word processor or desktop publishing package to write out their scripts.

If children use a word processor, show them how to use the formatting commands such as tabs and hanging indents to lay out their writing in the form of a dialogue. They should not use the space bar to move text around the screen. You may also need to set up hanging indents to make sure that the spoken text wraps around in the correct place and does not go back to the start of the line.

Lalo   Nanak, please come and eat at my house.
Nanak   Thank you. I would be very happy to eat with you.

The same effect can be created with a desktop publishing package by setting out two columns and typing directly into the columns. Some word processors also have a 'table' facility, which is very similar. This method is probably easier for the children to use once the columns have been set up.

| Lalo | Nanak, please come and eat at my house. |
| Nanak | Thank you. I would be very happy to eat with you. |

Assembly ideas

As part of an assembly focusing on a theme such as 'Wealth and riches' or 'Happiness is…', ask a child to open an envelope and read out a letter announcing that a relative is giving him or her a large sum of money. Another child could spring up and shout, 'You're rich, you lucky thing!' A third child could pose the question, 'Will it bring happiness?' Several children could then read extracts from the work carried out in the extension activity describing the positive and negative aspects of acquiring a large amount of money. Another child could explain that all religions have teachings on what wealth does to people. The story of Malik Bhago and Lalo could then either be acted or read. End the assembly with a reflection such as, 'And now, in a moment of quiet, let us think about what being wealthy means. It could be that real wealth is much more than pounds and pence.'

Reference to photocopiable sheet

Photocopiable page 114 gives a version of the Sikh Malik Bhago and Lalo story for the teacher's use. Copies could also be made for children who wish to refer to it when completing their tasks.

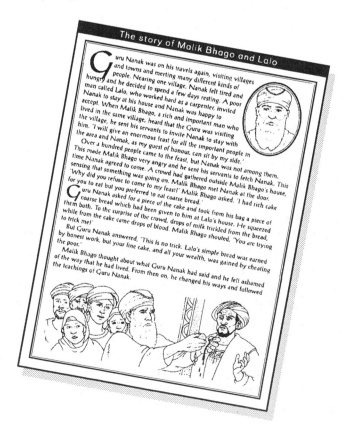

WHAT WOULD I REFUSE TO DENY?

To identify important personal beliefs or convictions. To understand that some people have such strong beliefs and convictions that they are willing to die for them.

Conviction. Belief.

†† *Individual followed by paired work, then whole class followed by individual work.*

🕐 *Individual 10 minutes; paired 10 minutes; whole class 30 minutes; individual 30 minutes.*

Key background information

This activity, which focuses on the role of beliefs and convictions, looks backwards, to the life of Bilal, and then at the contemporary world where strong beliefs and convictions can still demand a high personal price.

Bilal, a black Abyssinian slave before becoming a Muslim, is a much-admired person in Muslim history. He came to believe in the oneness of God (a belief which Muslims call *tawhid)* so strongly that, even under torture from his master, he refused to deny it. His courage and steadfastness led to him gaining his freedom and he became a companion of Muhammad, who gave him the honour of being the first *Mu'adhin* – the person who, calling out in Arabic, summons Muslims to prayer five times daily.

In later history, the call to prayer (*adhan*) was delivered from the minaret of the mosque. Recordings of the adhan are available (see 'Useful books and resources', page 109).

Preparation

Make copies of photocopiable page 115, one for each child. Become familiar with the story of Bilal on photocopiable page 116 and make copies for those children carrying out the support activity.

Resources needed

Photocopiable pages 115 and 116; writing materials.

What to do

Give each child a copy of photocopiable page 115 and explain that on the sheet there is a list of things that many people believe to be really important. Ask them to read through the list and choose five which they think are important. There is space on the sheet for children to add their own beliefs if they want to include these in the five. Once they have chosen five, they should put them in order from the most to the least important. Set a time limit for this task.

Each child should them compare her list of five beliefs with that of a friend, and spend some time talking about how their lists are similar and different.

Bring the class together and ask whether anyone would like to talk about their list and what they found when they compared it with a friend's.

Explain that there are some people who not only hold strong beliefs but who are willing to be put in prison, tortured or even prepared to die for them if they have to. Then tell the children that there is a Muslim story about a man called Bilal who was tortured for his beliefs but who refused to deny them. Read the story on photocopiable page 116 or ask a child to do so.

To complete the activity, give the children the choice of either:

▲ writing an imaginative story about a situation in which they find themselves having to defend their most important conviction (identified in the opening task);

▲ writing an extract from Bilal's diary about the circumstances which led him to give the first call to prayer.

Suggestion(s) for extension

Ask children to find out about people who have been imprisoned, tortured or killed for their beliefs.

Suggestion(s) for support

Children who find the activity difficult should be encouraged to choose the second option given at the end of the main activity. They may also find it helpful to refer to a copy of photocopiable page 116.

Assessment opportunities

Responses to the first task, together with the imaginative account written by some children, will provide evidence of the extent to which they are able to understand the significance of important personal beliefs. The extract from Bilal's diary and the research carried out in the extension activity will provide evidence of the extent to which the children understand that personal beliefs are so central to some people's identity that they are prepared to die for them.

RELIGIOUS EDUCATION

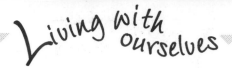
Opportunities for IT

Ask children to write their story or diary extract using a word processor. Those children who carry out the extension activity could use a CD-ROM to research information on people who have suffered for their beliefs.

Assembly ideas

As part of an assembly focusing on a theme such as 'Courage' or 'I believe in...', a narrator can explain how the first part of the activity was carried out. A number of children could say, in turn, 'I believe...' and then turn over a card on which they have written their most important belief or conviction. The story of Bilal could then be told together with, if appropriate, stories of other people who have been imprisoned, tortured or killed for their convictions. You may like to end the assembly with a reflection such as, 'And now, in a moment of quiet, let us think about those many people we know nothing about who, while we live in comfort, are in prison or in pain because of standing up for what they believe to be right.'

Reference to photocopiable sheets

Photocopiable page 115 lists a number of beliefs and convictions from which the children must choose several and prioritise them. Space is also provided for them to add their own beliefs if they choose to do so. Photocopiable page 116 gives the story of Bilal for the teacher's use and for some children to use as support. It can also be referred to during the assembly.

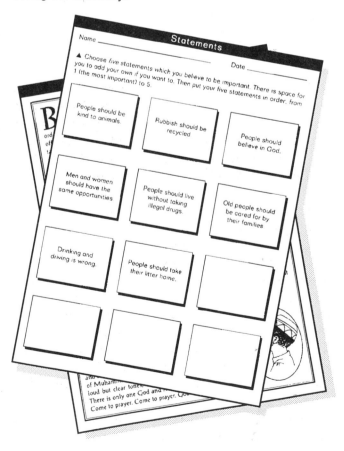

WHAT DO I THINK OF WHEN I HEAR THE WORD 'GOD'?

To encourage an interest in the role and range of beliefs and ideas. To understand that 'God' means different things to different people.

God. Belief.

†† *Whole class followed by group work, then returning to whole class.*

🕐 *Whole class 20 minutes; group work as appropriate; whole class 30 minutes.*

Key background information

It has been suggested that the nature of contemporary society encourages people to retain 'young' or 'childlike' images and ideas of religion which do not develop and mature: in time, they 'grow out of them' rather than 'grow into them'. This activity provides the opportunity for older junior age children to engage with and make sense of the range of ideas associated with the word 'God'. The small book *God-Talk with Young Children* by John M. Hull would provide useful background reading for the teacher as would *Exploring Inner Space* and *Religious Experience Today* by David Hay (see 'Useful books and resources', page 109).

As an activity appropriate for religious education, this activity focuses on how people respond when they hear the word 'God' rather than on whether people *should* believe in God. The activity as outlined cannot predict what the conclusions of the survey might be – but it could be that different responses according to the age, sex and family backgrounds of the respondents will be detected.

Preparation

Arrange with other classes for children to visit them in order to conduct the survey. To stimulate discussion about 'God', a story like 'God Knows' in *The Clothes Horse and Other Stories* (Janet and Alan Ahlberg, Puffin, 1989) may be useful.

Resources needed

Chalkboard/flip chart; clipboards; writing materials.

What to do

Gather the whole class together around the board. Ask for a volunteer scribe and ask the question, 'What do you think of when you hear the word "God"?' Encourage the children to speak as freely as possible and to include both positive and negative responses. Discuss, briefly, the range of ideas that is evident, noting the diversity as well as the similarities.

Explain that the aim of this activity is to find out what other people in school think of when they hear the word 'God'. Tell the children that, in groups, they are going to conduct a survey. They will need to think about who they

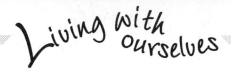

are going to ask and how they are going to record the responses. Arrange the children into groups and let them decide who they are going to approach. (For organisational purposes, it might be best if each group works with a different class or department in the school.) Check that no group has chosen the same class and set a time limit for the completion of the survey.

As the groups return, ask them to look at the responses that they have gathered and to come to a conclusion about what these responses tell them.

When all the groups have discussed their responses, gather the whole class together and ask each group to tell the others what they have found. When they have done this, examine with the children the similarities and differences between the findings of all the groups.

Suggestion(s) for extension
More able children could write to a number of people outside school, asking them what they think of when they hear the word 'God'. These could include local religious leaders, a local Member of Parliament, the Prime Minister, members of the Royal Family, sports and TV personalities.

Suggestion(s) for support
In order to support children who may find the activity difficult, ensure that the groups are of mixed ability.

Assessment opportunities
Listening to the responses from the groups as they report back to the whole class will suggest the extent to which the children have understood that 'God' means different things to different people.

Opportunities for IT
Ask children to use a word processor to write labels for the different responses to the word 'God' that they received. These can then be included in the class display.

The children could also analyse the range of responses received and try to group them in various categories. The information could then be displayed on a graph using a graphical package or used within a simple database.

Display ideas
The title 'We carried out a survey into what people think of when they hear the word "God"' could be placed at the centre of a display board. A range of responses to the question can be written on card and clustered around it in order to express diversity and range. Some of the conclusions drawn after the survey was carried out could be written up under a smaller heading 'What we learned from carrying out this survey'.

WHY DO I SOMETIMES NOT ACCEPT WHAT I KNOW TO BE TRUE?

To understand that the truth is sometimes hard to accept. To know that compassion is a central Buddhist teaching.

Truth. Compassion.

†† *Whole class followed by small group work returning to whole class.*

🕐 *Whole class 15 minutes; small group work 15 minutes; whole class discussion 15 minutes.*

Key background information
The state of enlightenment – seeing things as they really are – is central to Buddhism. The title *Buddha*, meaning 'Enlightened' or 'Awakened One', was given to the northern Indian prince, Siddhartha Gautama (*c.*563–483 BCE) after he reached enlightenment in his late twenties. He spent the remainder of his long life teaching others about how they, too, could take the path towards enlightenment. Within Buddhist teaching, wisdom and compassion complement each other; with greater awareness comes a sense of compassion for all other living beings.

The well-known story of the meeting between the Buddha and Kisagotami enshrines much that Buddhists hold to be true – that nothing is permanent, that clinging on to things causes suffering, that with awareness of the truth comes compassion. An animated version of the story is included in the video programme in the 'Buddhism for Key Stage 2' pack (see 'Useful books and resources', page 109).

Though a number of activities in the book suggest that religious artefacts are placed in a velvet or special bag, in this activity it is suggested that the Buddha image is *wrapped* in appropriate material. This is because the image can remain

RELIGIOUS EDUCATION

seated on the cloth when it has been unwrapped in order to emphasise its special status for Buddhists. The form of a particular image or statue (*rupa*) of the Buddha will be affected by the part of the world from which it comes as well as the quality of the Buddha it is portraying. The hand positions (*mudras*) are particularly important: hands slightly raised in front of the body, one above the other, indicate teaching; hands resting in the lap indicate meditation; hands touching the ground indicate the Buddha's confidence after he was Enlightened.

This activity shows how, in religious education, 'learning about religion' and 'learning from religion' can be held in a creative balance.

Preparation
Obtain a Buddha image (see 'Useful books and resources', page 109) and wrap it in a velvet or silk cloth. Make a copy of photocopiable page 117 and become familiar with the story of Kisagotami. Make copies of photocopiable page 118, one per group.

Resources needed
Buddha image velvet or silk cloth; photocopiable pages 117 and 118; writing materials.

What to do
Gather the children together and carefully unwrap the Buddha image. Place it where all the children can see it. Ask questions to encourage the children to look closely at the Buddha image.
▲ Do you think that this person is kind or unkind?
▲ Do you think that this person is angry or peaceful?
▲ What does the position of the hands tell you about what this person is doing?

▲ Would you like to meet this person?
Explain to the children that the image is of the Buddha and that for people called Buddhists he is very special because he was wise and could respond to other people's sufferings. He showed other people how they also could become wise and compassionate.

Tell the children that they are going to hear a story which tells of how the Buddha met a sad woman called Kisagotami. Read them the story.

Divide the children into groups, giving each group one copy of photocopiable page 118. Ask each group to choose a scribe whose role will be to record their group's responses to the questions. Set the groups a time limit for this task.

After the prescribed time, bring the groups together as a whole class and ask the scribes, in turn, to report on their group's responses to the final question.

Explain to the children that the Buddha taught that it is important to respond to the sufferings of others. Buddhists call this being compassionate. Kisagotami learned compassion when she understood that although she was grieving because her baby was dead, everyone else had felt sadness when people they loved had died.

Suggestion(s) for extension
Ask children to write an account of a time when they found it hard to accept something which had happened. How did they eventually come to accept it?

Suggestion(s) for support
Less able children could be given the support of their peers by making the small groups mixed ability. Alternatively, group less able children together and give them additional teacher support.

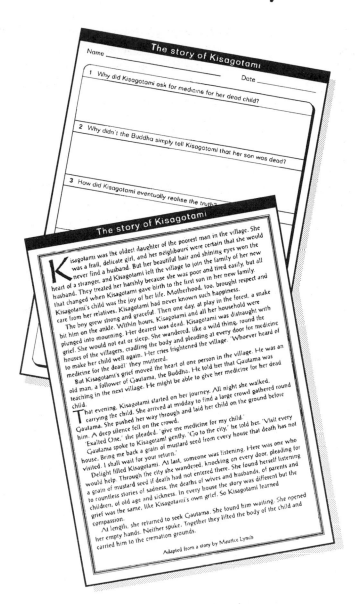

The story of Kisagotami

Name _____ Date _____

1 Why did Kisagotami ask for medicine for her dead child?

2 Why didn't the Buddha simply tell Kisagotami that her son was dead?

3 How did Kisagotami eventually realise the truth?

The story of Kisagotami

Kisagotami was the oldest daughter of the poorest man in the village. She was a frail, delicate girl, and her neighbours were certain that she would never find a husband. But her beautiful hair and shining eyes won the heart of a stranger, and Kisagotami left the village to join the family of her new husband. They treated her harshly because she was poor and tired easily, but all that changed when Kisagotami gave birth to the first son in her new family. Motherhood, too, brought respect and care from her relatives. Kisagotami's child was the joy of her life.

The boy grew strong and graceful. Then one day, at play in the forest, a snake bit him on the ankle. Within hours, Kisagotami had never known such happiness. plunged into mourning. Her dearest was dead, and all her household were grief. She would not eat or sleep. She wandered, like a wild thing, round the houses of the villagers, cradling the body and pleading at every door for medicine to make her child well again. Her cries frightened the village. 'Whoever heard of medicine for the dead!' they muttered.

But Kisagotami's grief moved the heart of one person in the village. He was an old man, a follower of Gautama, the Buddha. He told her that Gautama was teaching in the next village. He might be able to give her medicine for her dead child.

That evening, Kisagotami started on her journey. All night she walked, carrying the child. She arrived at midday to find a large crowd gathered round Gautama. She pushed her way through and laid her child on the ground before him. A deep silence fell on the crowd.

'Exalted One,' she pleaded, 'give me medicine for my child.'

Gautama spoke to Kisagotami gently. 'Go to the city,' he told her. 'Visit every house. Bring me back a grain of mustard seed from every house that death has not visited. I shall wait for your return.'

Delight filled Kisagotami. At last, someone was listening. Here was one who would help. Through the city she wandered, knocking on every door, pleading for a grain of mustard seed if death had not entered there. She found herself listening to countless stories of sadness, the deaths of wives and husbands, of parents and children, of old age and sickness. In every house the story was different but the grief was the same, like Kisagotami's own grief. So Kisagotami learned compassion.

At length, she returned to seek Gautama. She found him waiting. She opened her empty hands. Neither spoke. Together they lifted the body of the child and carried him to the cremation grounds.

Adapted from a story by Maurice Lynch

Opportunities for IT

Let the children use a word processor to write the labels for the display. Show them how to experiment with different fonts and sizes to ensure that the labels can be read from a distance.

Display ideas

Place the Buddha image on the velvet or silk cloth in front of a display board together with some mustard seeds (if available). Display a copy of the story on the board. Mount the first four questions from photocopiable page 118 on to separate pieces of paper and display them on the board. Surround each question with some of the responses from the groups. Give the whole display a title such as 'The Buddha meets Kisagotami. A story about compassion'.

Reference to photocopiable sheets

Photocopiable page 117 gives a version of the story used in this activity. Photocopiable page 118 contains five questions for each of the groups to discuss.

WHEN AM I TEMPTED?

To understand that being tempted is a significant human experience. To know about an episode in the life of Jesus.

Right. Wrong.

†† *Groups followed by whole class and then individual work.*

🕐 *Groups 15 minutes; whole class 30 minutes; individual work 20 minutes.*

Key background information

Three of the four Gospel writers whose Gospels begin the New Testament include an account of Jesus' 'Temptations'. The account given by Mark (chapter 1, verses 12–13) is very short. Those written later by Matthew (chapter 4, verses 1–11) and Luke (chapter 4, verses 1–13) are much longer. They are highly coloured or heavily influenced by the conventions and thought-forms of the day. The term '40 days and 40 nights', for example, meant a long period rather than a precise allocation of time.

The traditional understanding of Jesus' temptations is that they portrayed the choices which he would have had to have faced immediately before setting out on his public life (his 'ministry'). Was he to provide for people's material needs, perform startling deeds or serve evil instead of good? The devil – the tempter – personifies the lure of the choices which he faced and rejected.

If a less scriptural and more colloquial account of the temptations is preferred, this can be found in *Bible Stories for Classroom and Assembly: The New Testament*, by Jack G. Priestley (see 'Useful books and resources', page 109).

In giving the children the opportunity to reflect on what motivates them and the choices they have to make, this activity could make a contribution to their spiritual and moral development.

Tell the children that, in the New Testament part of the Bible, a story is told about how Jesus was faced with a number of temptations. These temptations took place at an important stage in his life. He had just left home and believed that he had a mission to tell and show people what God was really like. He went to a rocky desert area to think about how he was going to carry out his mission. It was while he was there, according to the Bible, that the devil showed Jesus three different sorts of temptation. Read the children the story from Matthew's Gospel and ask questions to encourage them to elicit the meaning from the story:
▲ Why do you think Jesus fasted?
▲ How did Jesus answer the devil after each temptation?
▲ What were the temptations?

Ask each child to choose one of the pictures from the photocopiable sheet and to write a short story explaining how a person faced the temptation shown in the picture and managed to resist it. They should attempt to put thoughts into words in as much detail as possible. If they wish, they can introduce a 'tempter' who engages in conversation with the person being tempted.

Suggestion(s) for extension
Make available the three different Gospel accounts of Jesus' temptations (see 'Key background information') and ask the children to compare and contrast the varying accounts.

Preparation
Make copies of photocopiable page 119, one for each child. Become familiar with the account of the temptations of Jesus in Matthew's Gospel.

Resources needed
Photocopiable page 119; writing materials. For the extension activity – children's Bibles.

What to do
Divide the class into groups and explain to the children that you want them to think about situations in everyday life when people are faced with temptation. (Make sure that the children understand what the word 'temptation' means.) Give each child a copy of photocopiable page 119 and ask each group to look at each picture in turn and talk about the temptation it depicts.

Then bring the class together and ask each group to talk about a different picture. Discuss any differences which may have arisen in the groups' ideas about the temptations portrayed in the pictures. Ask for volunteers to talk about any personal experiences of temptation.

Temptations

Suggestion(s) for support
If children have difficulty with the written account, ask them to cut out the relevant picture from the photocopiable sheet and write sentences about it.

Assessment opportunities
The responses from the groups as well as the quality of the individual written accounts will provide evidence of the extent to which the children understand that temptation is a significant human experience. Children could be asked about the biblical episode at a later time in order to see how much detail they have retained.

Reference to photocopiable sheet
Photocopiable page 119 depicts six situations, each of which could give rise to temptation. It is used by groups at the beginning of the activity to focus on temptation within human experience. It is used again at the end of the activity as a prompt for the individual written accounts.

Living with others

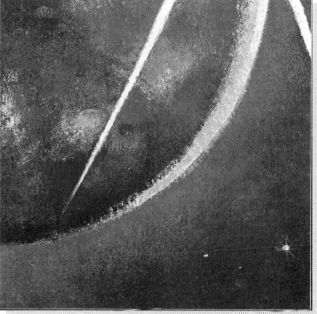

Human beings are profoundly social creatures. Our understanding of the world and our place within it is mediated to us by others – the family group, the society within which we live, the media, and so on. Though novelists, dramatists and film-makers continue to be fascinated with the 'loner', that term itself is socially conveyed. For most, it is the relationship with others that brings both the best of times and the worst of times.

This chapter gives children the opportunity to explore and respond to a number of social experiences which give rise to questions of meaning and value. These experiences are often deeply significant for the person and subtle in nature, such as coming to terms with the different 'world' of other people's homes, learning that possessiveness in relationships can have consequences for all parties, and that a personal response to the meanness or ill will of others can change the inner dynamic of the situation itself.

In order to provide a context in which these issues can be explored and responded to, all the activities use story. Some of the stories – such as the much-loved parable of the Good Samaritan and the Hindu story of Krishna the butter-thief – are drawn from religious traditions. Others are not overtly religious in character though their underlying themes are such that they can serve well the purposes of religious education.

WHY DID JESUS TELL THE STORY OF THE GOOD SAMARITAN?

To know one of Jesus' parables. To understand that love of others is a central Christian teaching.

Christian love. Parable.

†† *Whole class followed by group work, returning to whole class and ending with group work.*
🕐 *Whole class 20 minutes; group work 10 minutes; whole class 20 minutes; group work 20 minutes.*

Key background information

Interestingly, of the four Gospel writers it was only Luke who recorded this parable (chapter 10, verses 25–37). The setting of the story as described by Luke shows how Jesus' parables were typically told as a response to a particular situation. In this case, a Jewish legal expert asked Jesus what he had to do to achieve 'eternal life' – a question which was often discussed by earnest Jews of the day. (The retelling of the incident on photocopiable pages 120 and 121 puts the question into terms which children today may more easily understand.) Jesus responded by asking a counter-question which the man answered admirably – using two quotations from the Jewish *Torah*. Having answered his own question and perhaps to save face, the man asked a further question about who the term 'neighbour' applied to. It was in response to this further question that Jesus told the parable.

Within the Christian tradition, the parable has been explained in a number of ways, but for most Christians it points to the need for love of others – Christians often use the Greek word *agape* (pronounced 'a-gap-ay') to describe this kind of unconditional love in which the best is wanted for the other person, regardless of whether one feels personally drawn towards that person or not.

An excellent retelling of the parable of the Good Samaritan, together with background notes and teaching ideas, can be found in *Bible Stories for Classroom and Assembly: The New Testament* by Jack G. Priestley (see 'Useful books and resources', page 109).

Preparation

Make a copy of photocopiable pages 120 and 121 to read to the children. Make copies for each group.

Resources needed

Photocopiable pages 120 and 121; writing materials.

What to do

Explain to the whole class that you are going to tell them one of the most well-known stories told by Jesus, one which Christians think is very important. Before reading or telling the story, place it in context by giving the children background information about the geographical setting and the characters in the story. The parable used a well-known geographical location. The road from Jerusalem to Jericho, which dropped some 3600 feet in slightly less than 20 miles, was notorious for robbers and brigands. For Jesus' original audience, the fact that the person who did the 'right thing' was a heretic –

there had been enmity between Jews and Samaritans for five centuries – was important. The priest and the Levite were both Jews who assisted in the religious activities centred on the Temple in Jerusalem. For them to touch a dead body would have meant that they were made unclean and could not carry out their duties at the Temple.

Next, explain that Jesus told many stories called parables. These were told in response to a particular situation, such as someone asking a question, and were used to encourage people to focus on how they lived their lives.

Tell or read the story of the Good Samaritan on photocopiable pages 120 and 121, including the context given above surrounding the telling of the story. Then divide the children into groups (you may like to do this on an ability basis) and ask each group to consider the following three questions and to record their answers on paper:

▲ Why did Jesus tell this story in answer to the question, 'Who is my neighbour?'

▲ What would the story make people think about in their own lives?

▲ Why do Christians think that the story is so important?

Set a time limit for the completion of this task.

Bring the whole class back together and give each group the opportunity to report back. Having heard and discussed their answers, emphasise that the story is important to Christians because it reminds them that they should show love to all people, in the sense of wanting the best for them. Explain further that 'loving' someone in this sense is not necessarily the same as 'liking' them.

Returning to their groups, and in order to consolidate their knowledge of the story, the children can then devise and rehearse a dramatic interpretation of the parable. This could include the circumstances in which it was told. Give each group a copy of photocopiable pages 120 and 121 for them to refer to while they are planning their plays. Each group can perform their interpretation to the rest of the class at different times during the following week.

Suggestion(s) for extension

Ask children to write either a summary of the story told by Jesus or their own version of the parable, using modern-day characters and a known geographical location.

Suggestion(s) for support

Less able children, working as a group, can be given support from the teacher when answering the questions.

Assessment opportunities

Watching the children's performances of the play will provide evidence of their knowledge and understanding of the parable.

Assembly ideas

As part of an assembly focusing on a theme such as 'Stories that Jesus told' or 'Living with others', ask a narrator to explain the circumstances which led to the telling of the parable. Two groups can then perform their interpretations. Children who had carried out the extension activity could read out their modern-day versions. Finally, a child could explain why the parable of the Good Samaritan is so important to Christians. You may like to end the assembly with a reflection such as, 'And now, in a moment of quiet, let us think about times when we meet people who need our attention or support. Will we be the one who walks by on the other side or will we be like the Samaritan who stopped and spent his time, emotions and money on the unfortunate person who had been robbed?'

Reference to photocopiable sheets

Photocopiable pages 120 and 121 give a version of the parable of the Good Samaritan for the teacher's use and also for the groups to refer to when devising their plays.

RELIGIOUS EDUCATION

HOW ARE FAMILY MEMORIES SOMETIMES EVOKED?

To understand that memories can be evoked by physical objects. To develop the capacity to reflect on relationships and past experiences.

Symbolism. Family.

👥 *Whole class followed by individual work.*

🕐 *Whole class 30 minutes; individual work 30 minutes.*

Key background information

Communities, whether families, schools, religious groups or nations, are to a significant degree what they are because of shared memories. Such memories are recalled and made present in a number of ways, such as through storytelling, ritual, festival and physical objects.

As well as giving children the opportunity to reflect on their own family traditions, this activity also develops the awareness that physical objects can be powerful carriers of meaning and memory. This, in turn, will help them to understand many aspects of religious practice. Through providing another perspective – the symbolic – this activity would complement work related to the programme of study for science 'Materials and their properties'.

Preparation

Find a number of things made from fabric which remind you of people, events or things in your family. These could include:

▲ an embroidered tablecloth – memories of your grandmother;

▲ a blanket from a nursery – memories of your own, or your child's, first years;

▲ a school tie – your days at school;

▲ a veil – your wedding day;

▲ a college scarf – your days as a student.

Become familiar with the story of *The Patchwork Quilt* by Valerie Flournoy (Picture Puffin, 1995).

Resources needed

Examples of fabric (see 'Preparation'); a copy of *The Patchwork Quilt*; enough pieces of paper for two per child; writing and drawing materials.

What to do

Sit the children in a circle so that they can all see you clearly. Explain that you are going to show them some things made of fabric which, for you personally, are reminders of people,

events or times in your family. Hold up each item individually and talk about the significance it holds for you.

Next, ask the children if they can think of any items made from fabric which remind them of people, events or times in their families. As the children give examples ask them to describe what the fabric looks like, and who or what it reminds them of and why.

After you have heard several examples, tell the children that you are going to read them a story about a grandmother who, with her granddaughter and other members of the family, made a large patchwork quilt out of squares of lots of different kinds of material. Read the story of *The Patchwork Quilt*.

Give each child two pieces of paper and ask them to fold each one so that it is divided into eight panels. Ask the children to think about eight items made of fabric which remind them of people, events or times in their own families. On one piece of paper they should draw a picture of what the fabric looks like so that they end up with their own 'patchwork quilt'. Using the other piece of paper, they should then produce a 'key' in which they indicate what the fabric is in each panel and what it is a reminder of.

Suggestion(s) for extension

Children requiring extension work can be asked to choose one of the panels from the 'patchwork quilt' and expand the explanation given in their 'key' into a short story.

Suggestion(s) for support

If children experience difficulty with the main activity, ask them to fold their paper into four, rather than eight, panels. This will give them more space to draw their items and require fewer written explanations.

Assessment opportunities

The 'patchwork quilts' and associated 'keys' produced by the children will give a general indication of the extent to which they have understood that memories can be evoked by physical objects.

Opportunities for IT

Let the children use an art package to create their own range of patterns for the patchwork quilt. Using the art package tools show them how to explore the use of colour, tone, shading and pattern to create their own 'printed' version of the materials used in a patchwork quilt, such as velvet or corduroy. (You will need a colour printer to complete this task.)

Display ideas

Mount a patchwork display under a general title such as 'We thought about how things made from fabric often remind us of our families'. This can consist both of squares of real fabric and the children's drawings and written work.

DO SISTERS AND BROTHERS EVER UNDERSTAND EACH OTHER?

To develop the capacity to reflect on relationships. To develop the ability to empathise with others.

Relationships. Fairness.

†† *Group work followed by whole class and ending with paired work.*

⊕ *Group work 10 minutes; whole class 20 minutes; paired work 20 minutes.*

Key background information

Though this activity includes no explicit religious material, it provides the opportunity for children to progress in religious education by exercising skills related to the development of empathy. Such skills include, according to the SCAA model syllabus documents, 'the ability to consider the thoughts, feelings, experiences, attitudes, beliefs and values of others' and 'the ability to see the world through the eyes of others, and to see issues from their point of view' (see Introduction, page 8).

Preparation

Arrange groups so that they include some children who have brothers and sisters. Become familiar with *The Pain and the Great One* by Judy Blume (Piper Picture Books, 1988). Make enough copies of photocopiable page 122 for one per pair.

Resources needed

The Pain and the Great One; photocopiable page 122; blank speech bubbles; chalkboard/flip chart; writing materials.

What to do

Divide the children into groups and give each group the task of thinking of ten words which describe how brothers and sisters behave towards each other. Some examples can be given to start the children off, for example; 'kind', 'unfair', 'help', 'shout', but be careful to include both positive and negative examples. Tell each group to choose a scribe and set a time limit for the completion of the task.

After the allotted time, bring the whole class together and ask the scribe in each group to report back. As the words are read out, write them up on the board under either 'positive' or 'negative'. When all the words have been recorded, look at the balance between positive and negative and ask the children questions to encourage them to reflect further on the relationship between brothers and sisters.
▲ Why are there more words on the positive/negative side?
▲ What kinds of thing do sisters and brothers usually argue about?

RELIGIOUS
EDUCATION

▲ Are sisters and brothers similar deep down?
▲ Do children think that their mum or dad treats them in exactly the same way as their brothers and sisters?
▲ When are sisters and brothers kind to each other?

Next, explain that you are going to read them a story which is written in two halves about a sister and a brother. The first half is told by the eight-year-old sister who talks about her brother, whom she calls 'the Pain'. The second half is told by the six-year-old brother who talks about his sister, whom he calls 'the Great One'. Read the story.

Divide the children into boy/girl pairs of similar ability. Give each pair a copy of photocopiable page 122 and six speech bubbles. Ask the boy to be the brother and the girl to be the sister and to take turns to write what they think each character is saying. If there are uneven numbers the children can work in groups of three.

Suggestion(s) for extension

On a separate sheet of paper ask the children to write a story about an unjust incident in which a character says 'It's not fair!'

Suggestion(s) for support

Children who experience difficulty with the activity may find it helpful to work with a support teacher who can give them extra assistance.

Assessment opportunities

Listening to the children's answers to the questions about brothers and sisters will give some indication of the extent to which they are able to reflect on relationships. The completed speech bubbles with reference to photocopiable page 122 may also provide evidence of the extent to which the children are able to empathise with others.

Assembly ideas

As part of an assembly focusing on a theme such as 'Families' or 'It's not fair!', let one child ask the question, 'Do brothers and sisters ever understand each other?' Then ask other children to stand up, in turn, saying a sentence which includes either positive or negative words from the list compiled in the activity. For example, 'My sister is kind to me', 'My brother gets cross with me'. After one child has explained that the class looked at the book *The Pain and the Great One*, a boy and a girl can read extracts from the two halves of the book alternately, ending with the final section from each half. The question 'Do brothers and sisters ever understand each other?' is posed again, the assembly ending with a reflection such as, 'And now, in a moment of quiet, let us reflect on how easy it is to see only one side of a story – our own. Help us to stop and think more often so that we can understand the other person.'

Reference to photocopiable sheet

Photocopiable page 122 provides a series of pictures of brothers and sisters. In mixed pairs the children discuss each picture and then write text in accompanying speech bubbles.

WHY DO PEOPLE STILL LOVE US WHEN WE'RE NAUGHTY?

To know a story from the Hindu tradition. To identify a range of feelings associated with naughtiness.

Childhood. Love.

†† *Small groups followed by whole class, then individual work ending with whole class.*

⏲ *Small groups 15 minutes; whole class 20 minutes; individual work 30 minutes; whole class 15 minutes.*

Key background information

In that this activity touches on an experience that children love to talk about – being naughty – it is a simple one. Yet in at least two other ways it is a subtle and difficult activity.

First, on the level of human experience, it involves an exploration of an emotional response for which there is no effective word in the English language: the feeling of being both annoyed and delighted, *at one and the same time*, so that even when a child is being naughty, parents can still admire the spirit shown by him or her. (Compare another feeling for which there is no single expression in English – taking pleasure in another's misfortunes – for which we have to use the German word 'schadenfreude'.)

Secondly, the activity draws on a story from Hinduism, within which the variety of belief and practice can be baffling for Westerners.

Krishna is believed to have been an appearance (*avatar*) of Vishnu, the supreme deity, who has appeared on earth on many occasions at times of need in order to restore goodness.

Hindus tell stories about different times in Krishna's life: his birth, his boyhood, his youth, and so on. What is distinctive about the childhood and youth stories is the frequent element of play and naughtiness. Even the Divine, then, has a sense of fun and games!

Many Hindus have a particular devotion to Krishna, who is referred to as 'Lord Krishna'. In statues and art, Krishna is usually shown as blue-skinned and holding a flute. Many Hindu temples and homes have pictures of baby Krishna, sometimes with his brother Balarama, stealing butter from their mother's butter pot. Small three-dimensional images of 'Bal Krishna' (baby Krishna) are sometimes used to aid devotion.

Preparation

Make copies of photocopiable page 123 and become familiar with the story of Krishna, the butter-thief.

Resources needed

Photocopiable page 123; writing materials.

What to do

Divide the class into small groups and ask each child to tell the rest of their group about a time when they were naughty. They should include other people's reactions and the consequences of what they did. Give the groups a time limit to complete this task.

Bring the class back together and explain that many Hindus believe that the god Krishna did naughty things when he was small, but that his mother, Yashoda, loved him even though he was naughty. Tell or read the story of Krishna, the butter-thief on photocopiable page 123.

Ask questions to encourage the children to focus on the range of feelings felt by Yashoda when Krishna was naughty.
▲ Was Yashoda cross with Krishna?
▲ Why did Yashoda smile even though she was cross?
▲ Why did Yashoda forgive Krishna?
▲ Do you think that Krishna stole the butter again?
Tell the children that you would like them to write a story about a time when they did something naughty which didn't hurt anyone. They should include in their story how adults reacted to what they did. When the stories are finished, choose several children to read theirs to the class and talk about the different ways in which adults reacted. Come to the conclusion with the children that, even though we do naughty things, we are still loved.

Suggestion(s) for extension

Instead of writing an account of a time when they were naughty, ask children to imagine that they have a younger brother or sister who they find helping him or herself to cream from a container in the fridge. The child has cream around his or her mouth and is still holding the container. The children should write an account of what they do next and include how they feel towards their brother or sister.

Suggestion(s) for support

Children requiring support may need to discuss their example of naughtiness with you or a support teacher in order to clarify what the adult's reactions were.

Assessment opportunities

The children's written stories will indicate the extent to which they have been able to identify a range of feelings associated with bad behaviour.

Display ideas

Display the children's stories under the title 'Why do people still love us when we're naughty?' The Hindu story of Krishna, the butter-thief can also be displayed with the title 'Hindus love to hear stories about baby Krishna being naughty'.

Reference to photocopiable sheet.

Photocopiable page 123 is a retelling of the story about Krishna stealing the butter and should be told to the children during the activity.

Krishna, the butter-thief

Yashoda loved her baby son, Krishna. Whenever she wasn't working in the house, she spent time with him. One day, Yashoda was making butter. Krishna loved to watch his mother stir the milk with a big stick and hear the glugging noise as it began to change into butter. After a while, Krishna felt hungry and wanted to be fed. He tugged at Yashoda's sari and she left her churning to feed her baby son. Then, suddenly, she remembered a pan of milk she had left to boil and went to remove it from the heat. Krishna was angry and upset that his mother had left so suddenly. He looked at the pot of freshly churned butter. Then he pushed the pot over and it cracked into pieces on the hard floor. He put his hands into the butter and licked his fingers. When Yashoda returned, she saw Krishna with butter around his mouth and on his fingers and she saw the broken pot with her freshly churned butter spilling on to the hard floor. Although Yashoda was angry with Krishna for spoiling her butter and for breaking the pot, she couldn't help smiling as she looked at her son covered in butter. She knew he must be punished, but she loved him even more.

SHOULD YOU HELP AN ENEMY?

To interpret the teaching of a story from a religious tradition. To identify some of the consequences of different forms of behaviour towards others.

Relationship. Consequence.

†† *Paired work followed by whole class, then paired work ending with whole class.*

🕐 *Paired work 10 minutes; whole class 15 minutes; paired work 20 minutes; whole class 15 minutes.*

Key background information

Religious traditions usually include teaching about behaviour, particularly with regard to others. Indeed, some speak as though religion and morality are the same thing.

Within the Sikh tradition, the concept of *sewa* (pronounced 'say-va') is important. It refers to selfless action for the sake of others, irrespective of who they are. The well-known story of Bhai Ghanaya – *Bhai* (brother) is a term of honour for Sikhs – enshrines this teaching. The incident took place when Sikhs were fighting Muslims during the time of the tenth and last human Guru of the Sikhs, Guru Gobind Singh (1666–1708 CE).

The concept of sewa finds parallels in other religious traditions, such as the 'golden rule' ('Do to others as you would like them to do to you') in Christianity. But such teachings will almost certainly also find a parallel in a school's values and code of behaviour. As such, following up classroom work during assembly time is particularly appropriate here in that assembly or collective worship is the time when the school reminds itself of the values which it is seeking to perpetuate.

In giving children the opportunity to think about the personal consequences of their actions, this activity will make a contribution to their moral and social education.

Preparation

Make copies of photocopiable page 124, one for each pair.

Resources needed

Photocopiable page 124; writing materials.

What to do

Ask the children to work in pairs and give each pair a copy of photocopiable page 124. Ask them to read the story and then decide what this story teaches Sikhs about living a good life. Set a time limit, by the end of which each pair should have written a sentence to explain the teaching in the story. Bring the class together, listen to what each pair has written and agree on a sentence which best expresses the teaching in the story.

Explain that every day we encounter situations in which people can become our friends or enemies and the actions we take can often determine which they become. Give the children this example. You (a child) are walking into assembly with your class when a new child from another class trips you up deliberately and you almost fall. The new child laughs at you. Working in their pairs, ask the children to think up at least three different kinds of response to this situation. For instance, retaliate immediately with a kick, retaliate later with the help of some of your friends, tell a teacher, ignore what has happened or find the new child in the playground and try to be friends. Then they should try to decide which response is closest to the teaching in the Sikh story.

Finally, ask the pairs to evaluate the consequences each of their responses would have and then decide which course of action would be the best to take and why. Bring the children back together and share ideas as a whole class.

Suggestion(s) for extension
Children could find another example of a story from a religious tradition with a teaching similar to that in the water-carrier story, for example the Good Samaritan from the Christian tradition.

Suggestion(s) for support
Some children may need extra encouragement to think of positive courses of action in the later paired work.

Assessment opportunities
The sentence each pair is asked to write at the beginning of the activity should indicate whether the children have been able to distil the meaning of a story from a religious tradition. The children's responses to the situation which you pose to them and their identification of suitable and unsuitable consequences will provide evidence as to whether they have understood the consequences of different kinds of behaviour.

Opportunities for IT
Ask the children to use a word processor to write out their explanation of the teaching in the story. These can then be printed out and displayed around a copy of the story (this could be word-processed by another group of children). The final agreed class version can also be printed out for display alongside the others.

Assembly ideas
As part of an assembly focusing on a theme such as 'Friends and enemies' or 'Living with others', some children could act out a series of different responses to the school situation described in the activity. A narrator can then explain that, though it might be easier to respond in some ways than others, many religions teach that the right way to eliminate one's enemies is not by destroying them but by turning them into friends. The Sikh story of the water-carrier can be told to illustrate this point and reference could be made to stones from the Christian and other traditions. End the assembly with a reflection such as, 'And now, in a moment of quiet, let us think about situations when we have made enemies when, really, we could have made friends.'

Reference to photocopiable sheet
Photocopiable page 124 retells the story of the water-carrier for pairs to discuss and analyse at the start of the activity.

The water-carrier

The battle had been raging for several weeks. The Sikh fortress was under siege and soldiers from both sides had been killed and badly wounded.

At the end of each day, one man made his way through the dying and wounded on the battlefield. He carried a bag of water on his back and, kneeling by the side of each wounded soldier, offered a drink as well as words of comfort.

A group of Sikh soldiers had been watching the man for days. They were angry that the man, a Sikh, was helping not only the Sikh wounded but their enemies as well. Finally, they could stand it no longer and decided to report him to the Guru.

'Bhai Ghanaya is helping our enemy. He should be punished!' they told the Guru. The Guru looked troubled and he sent for Bhai Ghanaya.

'I have heard that you are helping the enemy,' said the Guru. 'Is this true!'

'When I help the wounded,' replied the Sikh, 'I don't see friends or enemies. I only see injured people who are in need.'

The Guru was silent for a moment and then, turning to those who had complained, said, 'This man is a true Sikh!'

He turned back to Bhai Ghanaya and, giving him some ointment, told him to carry on doing his good work and to use the ointment to ease the pain of all wounded people on the battlefield.

RELIGIOUS EDUCATION

WHY DO MY FRIENDS' HOUSES SEEM DIFFERENT TO MINE?

To understand that different people have different lifestyles. To develop the attitudes of fairness and respect.

Lifestyle. Diversity.

†† *Whole class followed by pairs and then individual work.*

🕐 *Whole class 20 minutes; pairs 15 minutes; individual work 25 minutes.*

Key background information

As children grow older, their sense of 'world' will broaden and they will become increasingly aware that their own lifestyle is one of many possibilities. Their work in religious education will focus increasingly on how beliefs and values influence and shape lifestyles. In providing the opportunity for children to develop an awareness of different lifestyles, this activity also touches on a number of attitudes, the development of which are central to religious education. Of those listed in the SCAA religious education model syllabuses, 'Fairness' (including 'readiness to look beyond surface impressions') and 'Respect' (including 'respecting those who have different beliefs and customs to one's own') are particularly relevant here.

Preparation

Obtain a copy of *I'll Take You to Mrs Cole!* by Nigel Gray and Michael Foreman (Andersen Press, 1985).

Resources needed

I'll Take You to Mrs Cole!; writing materials. For the support activity – drawing materials.

What to do

Gather the children together and explain that you are going to tell them a story which will encourage them to think about the different ways in which people live at home. Read the story and then ask questions to focus the children's thoughts on the concepts of lifestyle and diversity.

▲ Why was the boy frightened of Mrs Cole's house before he went there?

▲ What was different about Mrs Cole's house compared to his own?

▲ What did he like and not like about Mrs Cole's house?

▲ How would you have felt visiting Mrs Cole's house?

Ask the children to work with a friend and, in turn, to tell each other about their own house and what makes it into a home for them. As well as listening, the friend should ask questions to encourage their partner to identify some of the things that, because they are so used to them, they might forget to mention. Explain that when they have spent enough time on this task, the children should each write an account of what the boy in the story would experience on coming to their own house. Circulate during the paired and individual activities in order to encourage and ask further questions.

Suggestion(s) for extension

After they have completed their written accounts, ask children to think of a relative's house and to make a list of the ways in which it is similar and different to their own. For instance, 'People always wear slippers in my granny's house but not in mine.'

Suggestion(s) for support

If children experience difficulties, ask them to draw a series of pictures of the boy coming to their house (in the style of Michael Foreman's in *I'll Take You to Mrs Cole!*) rather than a written account.

Assessment opportunities

The kinds of question that children ask during the paired activity, together with their written account, will provide general evidence of the extent to which they have understood that different people have different lifestyles.

Opportunities for IT

Show the children how to use an art or drawing package to create a picture of a part of their house, either a room inside or the outside view. These pictures could be included within a word processed version of the visitor to their house. An alternative to drawing pictures would be to ask the children to bring in photographs from home which could be scanned, or for the children to create their own line drawings of their houses.

WHAT HAPPENS WHEN WE WANT TO KEEP PEOPLE TO OURSELVES?

To deepen an understanding of how relationships develop. To develop the ability to see the world through the eyes of others, and to see issues from their point of view.

Relationship. Jealousy.

†† *Whole class followed by large groups, then trios, ending with individual work.*

⏲ *Whole class 20 minutes; large groups 10 minutes; trios 10 minutes; individual work 20 minutes.*

Key background information

The story used in this activity could well be used as a stimulus for work in language or art, but it is the manner in which it is explored that makes it appropriate to work in religious education. The thrust is on exploring the nature of relationships from different perspectives. It also includes the opportunity for the children themselves to raise questions about value, belief and purpose.

In order to protect people's feelings and to maintain a positive mood, it might be appropriate to agree certain 'ground rules' before the opening discussion begins – that no reference should be made to people in the class, or to other people by name, for example.

In giving children the opportunity to reflect on relationships, this activity can make a contribution to their social development. In that relationships give rise to questions about what it means to be 'fully alive', this activity might also contribute to children's spiritual development.

Preparation

Become familiar with *John Brown, Rose and the Midnight Cat* by Jenny Wagner (Picture Puffin, 1985).

Resources needed

John Brown, Rose and the Midnight Cat; writing materials.

What to do

Gather the children together and introduce the theme of the activity – that sometimes people can be possessive about their relationships and can become jealous when friends try to get to know other people. Illustrate this, if possible, by examples from your own experience and then ask the children about examples from theirs.

Explain that you are going to tell them a story about an old lady and her dog and what happens when, one night, a cat appears. Ask them to be thinking of questions which they might raise about the feelings and reactions of each of

the characters in the story. Read *John Brown, Rose and the Midnight Cat.*

Through responding to the questions raised by the children, supplemented by your own, if necessary, explore the range of feelings illustrated in the story. Examples of such questions might be:

▲ Why did John Brown close the curtains?
▲ Why did John Brown tip the milk away?
▲ Why did the midnight cat keep coming back?
▲ Why did Rose stay in bed?

Divide the class into three evenly sized groups, each group representing one of the characters in the story. Explain that the groups' task is to discuss how their particular character feels during the story and why they do what they do. Each child in the group will need to keep notes of what is being discussed. Set a time limit for this task and move among the groups to listen to the discussions and to encourage or intervene as necessary.

At the end of the agreed time, regroup the children into threes, each trio consisting of a person representing one of the characters in the story. Referring to their notes, each person should in turn talk about their feelings and actions in the story. Give a time limit for this task.

Individually, the children should then choose one of the characters, probably, though not necessarily, the one they discussed in their large group, and using pictures and text, write the story from the perspective of this character.

Suggestion(s) for extension

Instead of focusing on one character only, children could write a brief narrative version of the story followed by an interview with each of the three characters in order to show their different perspectives on what happened.

Suggestion(s) for support

Some children may need further help from you or a support teacher in order to produce words and pictures which represent the experiences of one character. They might also find it useful to refer to the notes made by other children.

Assessment opportunities

The task completed by individuals will provide evidence of the extent to which they are developing the capacity to see the world through the eyes of others.

Opportunities for IT

Still working in their threes, ask the children to create a small booklet of the story using a word processor or desktop publishing package. The booklet could contain a written account of the full story, possibly including pictures drawn using an art package, and then each child's individual account written from the perspective of one character in the story. These can be printed out and published together.

An alternative approach would be to use a multimedia authoring package to create a more interactive presentation of the story and the character's feelings. The story could be rewritten over several pages (rather like a talking book). Each page could contain the text of the story, written by the children; illustrations which could be created using an art package or scanned from children's own line drawings; voices of the characters recorded using a microphone attached to the computer; backwards and forwards arrows to move through the story; and three icons to represent the characters in the story. The presentation could be set up so that when the reader clicks on one of the character icons they hear, or are shown, the views of the character at that particular point in the story. This is a fairly sophisticated approach and children using this type of software for the first time will need support.

Assembly ideas

As part of an assembly focusing on a theme such as 'Opening doors' or 'Living with others', the story of *John Brown, Rose and the Midnight Cat* can be told, followed by some of the children reading out their accounts of what happened from the perspective of each character. Interviews with the characters, drawing on the work carried out in the extension activity, could also be included. A song which develops the theme of life growing through loving relationships – such as *The Magic Penny* – could be sung. End the assembly with a reflection such as, 'And now, in a moment of quiet, let us think about the idea that, if we try to shut other people out, it makes us smaller inside and that a little bit of us dies each time we shut the door on other people. Help us, instead, to be the sorts of people who open doors and who grow big inside because of this.'

Living in the world

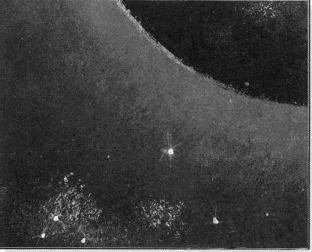

Human beings construct and inherit their own world of meanings and values but also live within the world of nature. This century has witnessed an increasing sensitivity to the 'environment' and awareness of the destructive as well as the creative role which human beings might play. Environmental issues have assumed an increasingly important place in the curriculum and culture of schools. 'Environmental education' has been identified as a cross-curricular theme within the National Curriculum and a grouping for subject areas within the Scottish 5–14 guidelines. Recycling bins are a common sight around schools and school children are often enthusiastically 'green'.

This chapter gives children the opportunity to explore a number of issues related to what is commonly called the 'natural world'. But it moves beyond this in providing opportunities for them to think about and reflect on how human beings themselves are *part* of nature and subject to its processes and rhythms. Many of the activities include references to religious material, such as the biblical story of Adam and Eve and the story of the Buddha's 'Four Sights'. But the thrust of the activities in general is towards encouraging children to make a response to the natural world – its use and abuse – and to express their responses in a variety of forms. They are asked to respond to pictures of trees and to an incident in which a ladybird is deliberately stamped on, for example. Forms of response include designing a 'new' world, writing verses of a song about harvest and planning a school 'Care for living things week'.

RELIGIOUS
EDUCATION

HOW WOULD YOU CREATE A WORLD?

To understand that people have always asked questions about how the world began. To form a judgement about what should or should not be included in a 'perfect' new world.

Creation. Ultimate question.

†† *Group work followed by whole class and then paired work.*

🕑 *Group work 10 minutes; whole class 15 minutes; paired work 30 minutes.*

Key background information

Evidence would suggest that questions of how (and why) the world began, and why it is as it is, have always fascinated human beings. Mythology and sacred texts contain many examples of stories and statements which offer answers to 'ultimate questions' concerning the origin and purpose of the world. It could also be said that, behind the scientific approach, there is the same desire and drive to find purpose, pattern and meaning.

Rather than looking at 'creation stories' as such, this activity offers children the opportunity to stand back from the world in which they have grown up and to consider what they would include and omit if they were creating a new world. Thus, the activity not only requires imagination but also discrimination and judgement, in that the children must distinguish between positive and negative aspects.

Preparation

Obtain an example of a creation story, if required. Examples of relevant collections include *Creation Stories* by Maurice Lynch (BFSS National RE Centre), *Creation Stories* by Jon Mayled (Wayland) and *Creation Stories: Anthology* by Angela Wood (Educational Television Company Ltd).

Resources needed

Example of a creation story (if appropriate); large sheets of sugar paper; marker pens; large sheets of plain paper; writing and drawing materials.

What to do

Divide the children into groups and ask each group to consider the question, 'How did the world begin?' A scribe from each group should record responses, which can be in the form of pictures as well as words. When they have finished, show each group's response to the whole class, asking scribes to explain briefly what ideas had been talked about in their groups.

Explain that, as far as we know, people have always asked questions about how the world began and why it is as it is. Different groups of people have had different ideas, which they have sometimes told as stories. Ask the children if they have ever heard any such stories. A story about creation could be told as an example (see 'Preparation').

Next, ask the children to imagine that they have the power to create a new world. They want this new world to be as perfect as possible, so they must think very carefully about what they will include in their new world and what they will leave out. The children should work with a partner and can use pictures and/or text on separate pieces of paper to show the features they would include and those they would omit when creating their new world.

Suggestion(s) for extension

Ask the children to find examples of creation stories from other religious and cultural traditions, such as Aboriginal, African, West Indian.

RELIGIOUS EDUCATION

WHY SHOULD WE LOOK AFTER THE EARTH?

To identify personal feelings towards Earth as a planet. To understand that there are a variety of responses to the use or abuse of the planet.

Wonder. Responsibility.

✝✝ *Whole class followed by individual work.*
🕐 *Whole class 30 minutes; individual work 20 minutes.*

Suggestion(s) for support
Children who find the activity difficult might benefit from discussing with an adult the good and bad aspects of the world in which they live.

Assessment opportunities
The response of the children to the first part of the activity will provide general evidence to indicate whether the children realise the emotive nature of creation theories. The final part of this activity will demonstrate to what extent children have been able to decide what should or should not be included in their 'new' world.

Opportunities for IT
Show the children how to use an art or drawing package to create a poster about their new world. Using pictures drawn with the software, or taken from the clip-art collections, they could show the items they would include or omit. They may also need to be shown how to add text and change the type size and colour so that they can describe aspects which cannot easily be shown.

Display ideas
Under a title such as 'Creating a perfect world', a large picture of a globe could be mounted and divided with a mark down the centre. One half could show features that children would wish to leave out of their new world, the other half features that children would like to include. Examples of creation stories from a range of religious and cultural traditions could also be displayed.

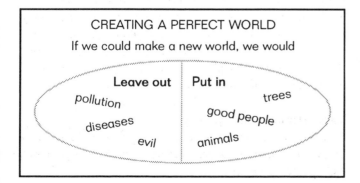

CREATING A PERFECT WORLD
If we could make a new world, we would

Leave out | Put in
pollution
diseases
evil
trees
good people
animals

Key background information
The astronomer Fred Hoyle said in the 1930s that once people had seen a picture of Earth from space, their image of themselves and their home planet would never be the same again.

This activity touches on what used to be called the 'awe and wonder' dimension of religious education. Though no explicitly religious material is included, it focuses upon an aspect of human experience which, for many, leads them into religious expression and response. There is much in the teachings of the major religions, particularly Christianity, Islam and Judaism, about human responsibility for the created world.

Preparation
Obtain a large picture of the Earth taken from space, together with a copy of *Dinosaurs and All That Rubbish* by Michael Foreman (Puffin, 1993). Make copies of photocopiable page 125, one for each child. Choose a piece of music to play during the first part of the activity, for example the Introduction to *Also Sprach Zarathustra* by Strauss (if applicable).

Resources needed
Dinosaurs and All That Rubbish; large picture of Earth from space; photocopiable page 125; piece of music (optional); chalkboard/flip chart; writing materials.

What to do
Gather the children together in a circle and explain that you want them to look at a picture showing the Earth from space. Pass the picture round the circle. (This can be done in silence or an excerpt of music could be played to increase the sense of atmosphere.) As the children look at the picture in turn, ask them to identify silently what it makes them feel or think about. Once all the children have had an opportunity to look at the picture, move round the circle again and record the response from each child on the board. Look at the list of responses and invite comments, for example about patterns of responses, or about those which are surprising. Some of the children might be asked to explain their particular responses.

Next, explain that you are going to read a story about how some people treat planet Earth. After reading the story *Dinosaurs and All That Rubbish*, ask questions in order to focus the children's responses.

▲ Why did the man want to reach the star?

▲ Why didn't the man stop the rubbish piling up?

▲ Why wasn't the man happy when he reached the star?

▲ Why did the man think that the Earth was paradise?

▲ Why didn't the dinosaurs want to keep the Earth for themselves?

Ask the children what they think the author's message was in the story. Prompt them if necessary – that we need to look after the Earth now, that we need to be grateful for what we have already, and so on. Decide on one statement which best incorporates the book's message and record it in the form of a statement (or statements if the children feel the book contains more than one important message). Store for later use in an assembly, if applicable.

Finally, give each child a copy of photocopiable page 125, explaining that in each box they should write what they imagine might have been some of the feelings and thoughts of the different characters in the book: the man before he travelled in the rocket, the people who worked in the factories, the man after he had returned to Earth, and the dinosaurs.

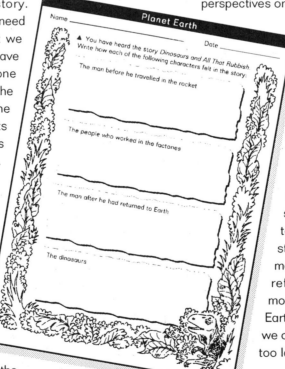

Suggestion(s) for extension

Ask children to continue the story of *Dinosaurs and All That Rubbish*, writing what they think might have happened next.

Suggestion(s) for support

Some children may find it helpful to refer to the book *Dinosaurs and All That Rubbish* to give them ideas when completing the photocopiable sheet.

Assessment opportunities

Listening to the types and quality of responses at the beginning of the activity will provide evidence of the extent to which the children are able to identify and verbalise their feelings about Earth. The completed photocopiable sheet will indicate to what extent children can identify a range of perspectives on how planet Earth should be treated.

Assembly ideas

As part of an assembly focusing on a theme such as 'Our world' or 'Planet Earth', the story of *Dinosaurs and All That Rubbish* could be read out, followed by 'interviews' with the man (before and after), a dinosaur and a factory worker. As a backdrop to this activity, the picture of the Earth from space could be mounted on a screen together with the message(s) of the story as agreed by the whole class. You may like to end the assembly with a reflection such as, 'And now, in a moment of quiet, let us think about planet Earth and remember that… (for example, we often only appreciate things when it is too late).'

Reference to photocopiable sheet

Photocopiable page 125 provides children with the opportunity to consider how different characters in the story of *Dinosaurs and All That Rubbish* might view what is happening to planet Earth.

WHY DO PEOPLE CARE FOR LIVING THINGS?

To know that some people care for living things for religious reasons. To encourage an attitude of respect for living things.

Ahimsa. Reverence for life.

†† *Whole class followed by group work returning to whole class and ending with group work.*

🕐 *Whole class 5 minutes; group work 5 minutes; whole class 15 minutes; group work 40 minutes.*

Key background information

The belief that there should be reverence for all living things is deeply embedded in Eastern religions. It finds its extreme exemplification in the Indian religion of Jainism. Jain monks and nuns wear masks over their mouths to prevent the accidental swallowing of insects and sweep the ground in front of them as they walk to avoid treading on living things.

In Hinduism, *ahimsa* is the title given to the doctrine of non-violence. This doctrine was brought to the notice of many in the West (including Martin Luther King) through the life of Mahatma Gandhi (1869–1948), who extended the doctrine to apply to achieving political ends through non-violent, passive resistance. The term 'reverence for life', however, was coined by the German Christian and medical missionary, Albert Schweitzer (1875–1965).

The cow is revered in Hinduism, and products which derive from the cow, such as milk and yoghurt, are believed to be pure.

The attempt to encourage an attitude of respect for living things in this activity is a particularly important but subtle one in that it touches on the bearing of people towards the world. It is obvious that reverence for living things cannot simply be 'taught', although this activity might provide the conditions in which seeds of this might be 'caught'.

Preparation

Obtain a picture of the Hindu god Krishna standing next to a cow (see 'Useful books and resources', page 109).

Resources needed

Picture of Krishna; large sheets of paper; scrap paper; writing and drawing materials.

What to do

Briefly tell the children about an imaginary occasion when a member of the class sees someone deliberately stamping on a ladybird and killing it. Divide the children into groups, asking each group to discuss their reactions to what you have just told them.

When the children have finished discussing the situation, gather the whole class together to listen to each group's response, exploring ideas and issues as appropriate.

Next, tell the children that various groups of people believe that all living things should be treated with care and respect. Hindus are one of these groups. Explain that the cow is a particularly important animal for Hindus and that, for example:
▲ the god Krishna is often shown standing next to a cow (show picture if available);
▲ cows can often be seen wandering streets and lanes in India – they are given the freedom to go wherever they want;
▲ milk from the cow plays an important part in Hindu worship and images of the gods are sometimes washed in milk;
▲ Hindus are usually vegetarian but would definitely not eat beef.

Divide the children into groups once again and set them the following task. You have decided that the class is going to have a 'Caring for living things week' with the aim of encouraging people in the school and the local community to respect living things more. Suggest that a picture of a ladybird is used as the logo for the week. Each group must agree on three activities which could be carried out during the week to promote this theme of concern towards living

RELIGIOUS
EDUCATION

things. These might include children giving a talk about how they look after their pets, holding a bring-and-buy sale to raise money for an animal charity, volunteering to lead a school assembly with the theme 'Looking after living things at school', drawing up a list of dos and don'ts for looking after things at school. In each case, the group should outline what will happen and how it will encourage respect for living things. Tell the children that, after they have decided, each group must design a poster to advertise the week in general and their three activities in particular.

Suggestion(s) for extension
Children who require extension work could be asked to carry out research into the place of the cow in Hinduism. This could include looking for photographs showing the cow in rural and urban Indian settings.

Suggestion(s) for support
Children who require most support with this activity may be those who have difficulty in acknowledging that respect should be shown to living things. These children will need greater teacher assistance and further discussion of the issues involved. It might be that something practical, such as making a wormery in order to observe the benefits which worms bring, is the most effective approach.

Assessment opportunities
Although the teacher will note the responses of the children to the various parts of this activity, the focus on attitudes means that anything but the most general form of assessment is inappropriate.

Opportunities for IT
Ask the children to use an art or drawing package to create a poster for their part of the 'Caring for living things week'. They could use a word processor to write their list of dos and don'ts for the care of living things. Tell the children to select appropriate fonts and to format the lists appropriately, for example increasing the type size, so that they can be displayed in the classroom.

Display ideas
Under a title such as 'Caring for living things week', mount the posters prepared by the groups. If the class carries out its activities, the display could be augmented with photographs and written reports. A smaller, separate display about how the cow is special for Hindus might be mounted and could include any photographs found by those children who carried out the extension activity.

RELIGIOUS
EDUCATION

WHY DO MANY CHRISTIANS SING SPECIAL HYMNS AT HARVEST TIME?

To identify key beliefs and ideas within a piece of Christian devotional writing. To identify and express some of their own ideas and beliefs about harvest.

Creation. Providence.

†† *Whole class followed by groups of about six children, returning to whole class and ending with individual work.*

🕐 *Whole class 20 minutes; group work 20 minutes; whole class 10 minutes; individual work 30 minutes.*

Key background information

It is difficult for most people living today to appreciate the importance that harvest time had for our forebears who largely lived in the countryside and off the land. Folklore and tradition echo with song, story and custom associated with harvest time as can be seen in books such as Bob Copper's *A Song for Every Season* and George Ewart Evans' *Ask the Fellows who Cut the Hay* (see 'Useful books and resources', page 109).

For Christians, with their belief in a Creator, it was natural that the 'hand of God' should be seen behind the processes of nature, including those leading to harvest. The harvest itself was a sign of *providence* – God providing caringly for his creation. A host of harvest hymns attest to these beliefs. 'We plough the fields and scatter', probably the most well known in England, was written by M. Claudius (1740–1815), who was German, and was translated into English by J.M. Campbell. It is full of colourful, anthropomorphic language (that is, language which uses human terms to speak of God) such as God 'painting the wayside flower' and 'lighting the evening star'. Some school hymn books or songbooks include more recent harvest hymns which refer to tractors and modern technology.

Though the 'home' of hymns is in devotional practice, this educational activity gives children the opportunity to explore words in order to find underlying beliefs and ideas. Among the 'skills and processes' which the SCAA model syllabus documents identify are 'investigation' (including 'knowing how to use different types of sources as a way of gathering information'), 'interpretation' (including 'the ability to suggest meanings of religious texts') and 'analysis' (including 'distinguishing between opinion, belief and fact'). The Scottish National Guidelines RE 5–14 also highlight understanding the purpose and content of Christian hymns (in Christianity: sacred places, worship and symbols).

Preparation

Identify a Christian harvest hymn, for example 'We plough the fields and scatter', and provide the words for the children to refer to when working in their groups.

Resources needed

The words of a Christian harvest hymn; writing materials. For the support activity – different coloured highlighter pens.

What to do

Gather the children together and ask them what they understand by the word 'harvest'. Explain that, when most people lived in villages and were dependent on the weather and local crops for food, harvest was a very important time in the year. A good harvest meant that people could look forward to the winter with confidence and, because they were relieved when the harvest was gathered in, they wanted to express their thanks and joy. Christians naturally did this by going to church to worship, and this included the singing of special hymns for harvest. Tell the children that they are going to look at a harvest hymn in order to find out what ideas and beliefs the person who wrote it held about God and harvest.

Look in detail at the first verse of a Christian harvest hymn, identifying key beliefs and ideas with the children. For instance:
▲ Humans plant but God provides the conditions for growth (warmth, rain, and so on).
▲ God 'lives' in heaven.
▲ Humans should be thankful to God.
▲ God is loving.

Divide the children into groups of about six, giving each group a copy of the words of the harvest hymn. Explain that their task is to read the rest of the hymn and then, verse by verse, to find out what the writer's beliefs about God and harvest time were. Tell the groups that they will need to share their ideas with the rest of the class at the end of a specified time. They may like to choose a scribe who can report back for the whole group.

At the end of the specified time, bring the whole class back together in order to hear and discuss the range of beliefs and ideas which the groups have identified within the rest of the harvest hymn. Write down the children's various suggestions as to the meaning of the hymn for distribution to those children carrying out the support activity.

RELIGIOUS EDUCATION

Finally, ask the children to write a verse or verses of a song which explains how they feel about harvest. This may or may not contain references to God.

Suggestion(s) for extension
Ask children to find another example of a Christian harvest hymn and compare it with the hymn looked at in the activity. What are the similarities and differences between them?

Suggestion(s) for support
Give children a list of the beliefs and ideas identified by the class and, taking each in turn, highlight with different colours the words or lines on the copy of the song which match particular ideas or beliefs.

Assessment opportunities
The results of the group work will provide evidence of the extent to which the children have been able to identify key beliefs and ideas in a Christian hymn. The extent to which the children have been able to identify their own feelings about harvest will be expressed in the verse or verses of their songs.

Opportunities for IT
Ask children to use the word processor to present their ideas about the key beliefs of the harvest hymn being studied. These can be printed out as labels to display alongside a copy of the hymn.

Display ideas
Under a heading such as 'Many Christians sing hymns at harvest time', the words of the harvest hymn used for the activity can be written out in large print. Key ideas and beliefs can then be written on paper or card and connected to the appropriate part of the hymn with ribbon or thread. Under another heading, such as 'Our beliefs and ideas about harvest', a selection of verses written by children could be displayed. Key ideas and beliefs contained in these might also be highlighted.

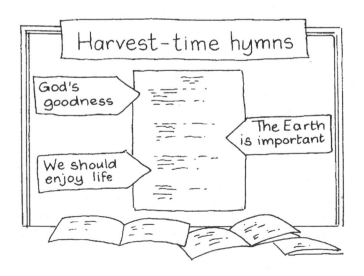

WHY DID ADAM AND EVE DISOBEY?

To know a story from the Judaeo-Christian tradition. To understand that story can convey truths about human nature.

Temptation. Symbolism.

†† *Whole class and then small group work, returning to whole class, then small groups again.*

🕐 *Whole class 5 minutes; small groups 20 minutes; whole class 20 minutes; small groups 20 minutes.*

Key background information
The story of Adam and Eve (Genesis, chapter 3) has had a profound effect on Christian thought in particular, and on Western culture in general. Many classic painters took it as a topic and the Garden of Eden scene has often been shown in stained glass. Interestingly, the original text says nothing about Eve plucking an *apple* from the tree – this idea developed later.

For Christians, the story of Adam and Eve's disobedience at the prompting of the serpent has been interpreted as depicting the 'Fall of Mankind' – the human situation in which, though the path of goodness is known, there is something deep within human nature which prevents people from following it through their own efforts.

RELIGIOUS
EDUCATION

Many Christians would now see the story as a 'myth', a story which contains truths without necessarily being literally true. As a myth, the story of Adam and Eve has been described as the story of 'Everyman' in that it portrays something fundamental about the nature of each and every person.

There are many retellings of this story. The Jewish storyteller David Kossoff included a version in his *Bible Stories*. Teachers will find particularly useful the retelling, background notes and teaching ideas in *Bible Stories for Classroom and Assembly: The Old Testament* by Jack G. Priestley (see 'Useful books and resources', page 109). Jack Priestley is well known for his contention that the story causes problems for adults rather than children.

Preparation
Make copies of photocopiable page 126, one for each child. Make copies of photocopiable page 127, one for each group of three. Find a picture depicting Adam and Eve if you wish to use this as a stimulus at the start of the activity.

Resources needed
A picture of Adam and Eve (optional); photocopiable pages 126 and 127; writing materials. For the extension activity – children's Bible.

What to do
Introduce the activity by asking the children what they know about Adam and Eve. If you have managed to obtain a picture of Adam and Eve show this to stimulate response. Explain that many people would say that the story of Adam and Eve is not about the first two people who lived but is about all of us and how we behave – it is a story which makes us think about ourselves.

Divide the children into groups of three. Give each child a copy of photocopiable page 126 and ask the children to read through the story of Adam and Eve. When they have finished, give each group a copy of photocopiable page 127 and ask them to discuss and answer the questions on the sheet. A scribe should record the group's responses. Set a time limit for this task and circulate among the groups to listen to their discussions and to encourage and prompt as necessary.

At the end of the prescribed time, bring the class back together and ask the scribes to report their group's responses. Discuss and develop each question where appropriate.

Ask the children to return to their group of three and to devise a role-play involving three characters: two people who have been told not to do something and a third character (not necessarily human) who persuades one of the people to do the forbidden thing. Explain that, when devising their role-play, they will need to identify:
▲ what the forbidden thing is;
▲ what form the tempter will take;
▲ how the tempter persuades one of the people to give in to the temptation;
▲ how one person persuades the other to do the forbidden thing.

End the activity by asking some of the groups to present their role-play to the rest of the class.

Suggestion(s) for extension
Ask children to look up the story of Adam and Eve in a Bible and, comparing it with the account on photocopiable page 126, to make a list of extra details which are found in the Bible's version.

Suggestion(s) for support
Children who find the activity difficult may benefit from the assistance of a teacher or support teacher when reading the story. They can then be asked to answer questions 2, 5, 6 and 7 on photocopiable page 127.

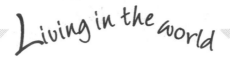

Assessment opportunities

Listening to the group discussions and watching the role-plays will indicate the extent to which the children have grasped that the story touches on aspects of human experience, such as feeling shame, doing wrong when the right action is known, apportioning blame rather than accepting responsibility.

Assembly ideas

As part of an assembly focusing on a theme such as 'Stories from the Bible' or 'Temptation', ask a narrator to recount a version of the Adam and Eve story. Some children could then explain some of the ideas which they think are contained within the story. Several of the role-plays could then be performed and the assembly could finish with a reflection such as, 'And now, in a moment of quiet, let us think about times when we know what we should do but something deep within us tugs us the other way. Help us to find the power to do what we know to be right.'

Reference to photocopiable sheets

Photocopiable page 127 provides a list of questions related to the Adam and Eve story. The children discuss these and then answer them with reference to the retelling of the story which is given on photocopiable page 126.

WHAT SIGHTS COULD MAKE US STOP AND THINK?

To know a key story connected with the life of the Buddha. To identify aspects of the world that give rise to ultimate questions.

Suffering. Meaning.

†† *Groups of four followed by whole class and then individual work.*

🕐 *Small groups 15 minutes; whole class 30 minutes; individual work as appropriate.*

Key background information

In both real life and literature, many stories have been told of people who lived contented lives of plenty until something happened that revealed that life was not so simple. It was time spent as a prisoner that led to St Francis leaving his merchant home in Assisi. In literature, both Voltaire's *Candide* and Oscar Wilde's *The Happy Prince* had their eyes opened in different ways.

A key Buddhist story tells of how Siddhartha Gautama was troubled by four sights and left home in order to find the cause and way out of pain and suffering. It was eventually to lead to his 'Enlightenment' (the title *Buddha* means 'Enlightened' or 'Awakened One') in which he saw the cause of suffering and the way out of it. Buddhists follow the path which he taught and demonstrated in his own later life.

This activity provides children with the opportunity to reflect on what experiences might challenge the notion that life is only about happiness and pleasure. In responding to this opportunity, they might raise 'ultimate questions' – questions about the meaning and purpose of life.

Preparation

Make copies of photocopiable page 128, one per group. Make a copy of photocopiable pages 129 and 130 and become familiar with the story. Collect together magazines and newspapers.

RELIGIOUS EDUCATION

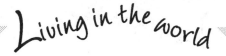
Resources needed

Photocopiable pages 128, 129 and 130; magazines and newspapers; writing and drawing materials.

What to do

Divide the children into groups of about four and give each group a copy of photocopiable page 128. Briefly go through the task, clarifying any queries which the children might have. Set a time limit for the task.

At the end of the time allowed, gather the whole class together and ask each of the groups to report back what they have written, explaining why each of their sights would make the person who had climbed over the wall stop and think.

Next, explain that you are going to tell them a story about a man called Siddhartha Gautama who is given the title 'the Buddha' by people called Buddhists. Tell them the story on photocopiable pages 129 and 130. Discuss why each of the four sights which Prince Siddhartha saw would have made him stop and think.

Tell the children that they are going to make a display about various aspects of the world which make people stop and think. Divide them into groups to work on each of the following display tasks:

▲ using magazines and newspapers to find pictures and articles;

▲ painting or drawing pictures of sights with a short written explanation;

▲ rewriting the story of Siddhartha Gautama in their own words;

▲ writing a modern imaginary story based on the photocopiable sheet used at the beginning of the activity.

Suggestion(s) for extension

Children requiring extension work should work on either of the last two display tasks. They should be asked to explain in writing what aspects of the Buddha's or their own story are challenging.

Suggestion(s) for support

The less able children should be asked to work on either of the first two display tasks. They may need prompting in order to identify those aspects of the world which give rise to ultimate questions.

Assessment opportunities

The setting of a written task or oral questioning some time after this activity will indicate to what extent the children have learned and remembered the story. The results of the initial exercise in this activity will provide evidence of the extent to which the children have been able to identify aspects of life which make them question the purpose and quality of their lives and those of others.

Opportunities for IT

Tell the children to use an encyclopaedia CD-ROM to research further information on the life of the Buddha. Alternatively, they could use a specific religious resource such as the Nelson *Media Aspects of Religion* CD-ROM.

Display ideas

Under a heading such as 'Sights that can make us stop and think', the material prepared by the four groups could be displayed in three sections: the story of Siddhartha, the modern imaginary tale, and magazine articles or pictures and children's artwork showing aspects of the world which raise ultimate questions.

RELIGIOUS EDUCATION

Reference to photocopiable sheets

Photocopiable page 128 gives an imaginary setting to encourage the children to think about sights which might challenge the assumption that life is easy and pleasurable. Photocopiable pages 129 and 130 provide the teacher with a retelling of the story of Siddhartha Gautama's four sights. Copies could also be given to assist those children writing the story in their own words.

WHY ARE TREES IMPORTANT TO PEOPLE?

To identify some of the ways in which trees are important to themselves and others. To understand how trees can become a focus of story and ritual.

Symbolism. Nature.

✝✝ *Session One: Whole class followed by large groups, returning to whole class and ending with single or paired work. Session Two: Whole class followed by individual work.*

🕐 *Session One: Whole class 10 minutes; large groups 15 minutes; whole class 20 minutes; single or paired work as appropriate. Session Two: Whole class 15 minutes; individual work 30 minutes.*

Key background information

Trees are such a common part of the natural landscape that it is easy to forget what an important grip they have had on the human imagination since earliest times. A glance at any large collection of photographs reveals how trees still become the focus of people's attention, if only through a camera lens.

Trees occupy an important place in folklore and folk religion; the Christmas tree has a long ancestry. Mythology is full of sacred groves and sacred trees, and it was often believed that trees had spirits.

Trees feature in the major religious traditions too. The tree has been a major symbol in Buddhism, for example. Buddhists and others who visit Bodhgaya in northern India – the place where it is believed Siddhartha Gautama achieved his Enlightenment – will often bring away heart-shaped leaves from the type of tree under which the Buddha sat. Sometimes images of the seated Buddha are outlined on these leaves. Some leaves are even painted with scenes from the Buddha's life.

RELIGIOUS EDUCATION

The minor Jewish festival of *Tu B'Shevat* (New Year for Trees) occurs each year on the 15th of Shevat, the eleventh Jewish month. It usually occurs in late January or early February. Many Jews try to eat fruit from Israel on that day, such as sharon fruit and oranges.

Preparation

Session One: obtain a picture showing a tree or trees to serve as a stimulus to start the activity. Become familiar with *The People Who Hugged The Trees* adapted by Deborah Lee Rose (Roberts Rinehart, 1990) if applicable. Prepare materials for individual/paired work. Session Two: become familiar with some examples of how trees figure in religion.

Resources needed

Session One: picture of tree or trees; large sheet of paper; *The People Who Hugged The Trees* (optional); writing and drawing materials. Session Two: writing materials.

What to do

Session One

Explain to the children that, for the next two sessions, they are going to be finding out some of the reasons why trees are important to people. Show the picture and ask them what they already know about trees. Listen to a few responses before dividing the class into four groups to play the tree game. Tell the children that the game is designed to encourage them to think about their *feelings* about trees.

Write the following starter sentences on the board:
Trees are...
If I were a tree, I would be a...
Trees make me think...
Trees make me feel...
If there were no trees, it would be...
When I touch a tree I feel...
The tree I like most is...

Tell the groups to choose one person to be the scribe. The scribe must allocate one of the statements to each person in their group. On a separate sheet of paper, each child in turn completes the statement they have been given and then reads it out to the scribe who should record on another sheet what has been said. Give a time limit for this part of the activity.

At the end of the time allowed, gather the whole class together and read through each statement, asking scribes to say how the person in their group completed it. Record all the suggestions on a large sheet of paper.

Next, extend ideas about why trees are important to many people. This could include:

▲ talking about those people who are prepared to go to great lengths to protect trees from harm or from being chopped down, such as protesters who spend many hours in trees in order to prevent them being felled when new roads are being built;

▲ reading the story *The People Who Hugged The Trees*;

▲ talking about how trees are sometimes planted as a memorial to people, perhaps a person closely related to someone in the school who has died.

Having discussed and developed any issues which arise, give the children the opportunity to develop their own ideas and responses further by choosing one of a number of activities which they can carry out singly or in pairs. You may like to suggest:

▲ painting a tree scene in such a way that it expresses their own feelings about trees;

▲ writing a poem about trees in general or a particular tree known to them;

▲ writing a newspaper article about a group of protesters who climb into trees in order to stop them being felled;

▲ writing a letter to a friend about a ceremony at school in which a cherry tree was planted to remember a special person who had died;

▲ doing a number of bark and/or leaf rubbings in order to show a variety of patterns, textures and marks.

Session Two

Begin this session by reminding the children of how important trees are to many people and explain that trees also play a part in many religious stories and traditions. Talk about one or two examples, including any that the children might themselves know.

▲ In the story of Adam and Eve in the Garden of Eden there were the tree of knowledge and the tree of life (see 'Why did Adam and Eve disobey?', page 44).

▲ Buddhists tell the story of how, 2500 years ago, a person called the Buddha sat under the bodhi tree and became Enlightened – understanding the meaning of everything (see 'Key background information' to 'What sights could make us stop and think?' page 46).

▲ There is a story which some Christians tell about three trees – one became the crib in which the baby Jesus was laid, one became a fishing boat in which Jesus stood to speak to the people on the shore and the third became the cross on which Jesus was crucified.

▲ Each year, Jews celebrate a minor festival called Tu B'Shevat, sometimes called the New Year for Trees, during which trees are planted in Israel and saplings and plants are sometimes taken to the synagogue to be blessed.

Go on to explain that some Jewish families who live in Israel plant a tree when a new baby is born into the family. As the baby grows and reaches different stages in life, the tree becomes the centre of various activities and ceremonies. For example, branches from it are used to decorate the canopy (*huppah*) under which the bride and groom stand when they get married.

Ask the children to imagine a person for whom a special tree was planted when they were born. They should identify at least three important times in the person's life. These might include going to school for the first time, having a

birthday, leaving home, getting married, a first child being born, becoming unemployed, changing jobs, and so on. The children should then think of a way in which, on each occasion, the tree could be used and why. When they have done this, they should:
▲ write a short account of what happens on each occasion;
▲ explain how the tree was used and why;
▲ illustrate the occasion.

Suggestion(s) for extension
Session One: differentiation (by aptitude and ability) is accounted for in this activity through the range and difficulty of tasks available. Children could choose to complete more than one task. Session Two: the more able children could conduct their own research into the importance of trees in folklore or in major religious traditions, such as the use of decorated fir trees, planting trees at Tu B'Shevat, and so on.

Suggestion(s) for support
Session One: differentiation is already accounted for in this activity through the range and difficulty of tasks available. However, some children may need advice about which activity is most suited to them. Session Two: some children may benefit further from discussion with an adult in order to

identify three important times and how the tree might be used, for instance when a person goes to school for the first time, a small branch of the tree could be taken to school and given to the teacher; at a birthday, the tree could be decorated and party games played next to it; when a person leaves home, they could take a cutting from the tree to plant in their new garden.

Assessment opportunities
In Session One the extent to which children are able to identify and express feelings and ideas evoked by trees will indicate whether they have understood the importance of trees in people's lives and societies. Be aware of those children who are able to identify three important times in a person's life and create ways in which trees might be a means of expressing the significance of each occasion.

Opportunities for IT
Allow the children to use an art or drawing package to create their own pictures of trees. They could try different line thicknesses and shapes to portray a tree in winter, or experiment with spray-can tools to add leaves to their picture.

Many of the writing tasks can be undertaken using a word processor or desktop publishing package. If children are using a word processor to write letters, show them how to use the formatting commands such as 'range right' to position

their address rather than using the space bar to move text around the screen.

Display ideas
Under the heading 'Why are trees important to people?', material which has been produced during this activity could be displayed, including the separate statements, with examples of different endings provided by the children, paintings, newspaper articles written by children, leaf and bark rubbings and the fruits of the research carried out by members of the extension group. In order to display the results of the last exercise, a timeline could be drawn and, at appropriate points, examples of rituals devised by the children shown.

Following guidance

If the concept of 'authority' is significant to human experience in general, it is central to religious traditions of all types and varieties. Authority implies something or someone greater than yourself which directs or influences the way you live and interpret the world, the seen and the unseen. The teacher in the classroom or the guru in the religious community (the word 'guru' itself means 'teacher') carry authority each in their own sphere and in their own way. The same could be said of a book of rules for a game and an ancient sacred text.

The activities in this chapter give children the opportunity to explore how following guidance is expressed in a number of religious contexts – within the biblical story of Jonah and through Sikh naming customs, for instance. Some of the activities develop learning by remaining within the religious context – by reflecting on what might anger Christians in the world today or by finding out about the role of the Five Pillars in the lives of Muslims, for example – while others move into the school world and the individual lives of the pupils. Identifying things which would unite two schools which are to be amalgamated or discussing the importance in life of public or personal promises are examples of the latter approach.

RELIGIOUS
EDUCATION

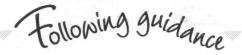

WHY DID JONAH CHANGE HIS MIND?

To know a story associated with a number of major religious traditions. To identify times in your own life when you have avoided following instructions.

Free will. Authority.

†† *Whole class followed by groups of about five, returning to whole class and ending with individual work.*
🕐 *Whole class 15 minutes; small groups 30 minutes; whole class 40 minutes; individual work 30 minutes.*

Key background information

Like Noah's ark, the story of Jonah has exerted a fascination on people's imagination, though there is no reference to a *whale* as such in the original version. The fish, in reality, is only a storyteller's device. It is a story with many layers of meaning and interpretation. The first Christians, with their belief in Jesus dying and rising on the third day, for example, immediately saw parallels with Jonah spending three days in the belly of the fish.

Historically, the story of Jonah (often described as a parable) was first told about 2500 years ago to counteract the tendency among some Jews of the time to be inward-looking in their religious views. God, the storyteller wanted to demonstrate, is greater than the Jews. Nineveh, a city which featured in the story of Jonah, was an ancient Assyrian city situated on the river Tigris which, for Jews, was a byword for wickedness.

The book of Jonah is included in the Christian Old Testament. Muslims believe that Jonah (in Arabic, Yunus) was one of the many prophets sent by God before the final prophet, Muhammad. He is referred to in the Qur'an, the longest reference being in *surah* (chapter) 37. His story is recounted by Jews during their solemn festival, Yom Kippur.

Preparation

Become familiar with the story of Jonah. Make copies of photocopiable page 131 – several copies per group.

Resources needed

Photocopiable page 131; writing and drawing materials.

What to do

Explain to the children that they are going to hear a story which was first told by people called Jews thousands of years ago and is found in a book in the Bible. Tell or read them the story. (Alternatively, you may like to ask a child to do this.) Ask questions to focus on key aspects of the story.

▲ Why did Jonah disobey God?
▲ Why didn't Jonah want to go to Nineveh?
▲ Why didn't Jonah want to pray for help during the storm?
▲ What made him pray for help when he was inside the big fish?
▲ Should God have asked Jonah a second time to go to Nineveh?

Divide the class into groups of about five children. Explain that the story is going to be split into three parts, these being:
▲ Jonah hearing the command to booking a place on board a boat;
▲ Jonah boarding the boat to being thrown overboard;
▲ Jonah being swallowed by the fish to hearing the command a second time.

RELIGIOUS EDUCATION

Tell the children that each group should focus on one part of the story only and prepare a presentation. Ensure that each part is worked on by at least two groups. Each group should agree on their own method of presenting their part of the story to the rest of the class. For example, they could choose drawings, paintings, poems, songs, drama or interviews. Give several copies of photocopiable page 131 to each group and specify a time limit for this section of the activity.

After the specified time, gather the children together again and, moving through the three parts of the story in sequence, ask each group to make a presentation to the rest of the class.

Finally, ask the children to think about a time in their own lives when they have been asked to do something which they have not wanted to do but have eventually done because something has happened to change their mind. They should either:
▲ write a narrative account of their experiences;
▲ present their experiences in a cartoon format.

Suggestion(s) for extension
Using reference books in the library, including the Bible, ask children to research what happened to Jonah when he reached Nineveh.

Jonah and the fish
One day, God spoke to Jonah and said, 'Go to the city of Nineveh and tell everyone who lives there that I have seen how wicked they are and that I want them to live better lives.'
Jonah said 'Yes God,' but he thought, 'I don't want to go to Nineveh where everyone is unkind. I will go somewhere else and God will never know.'
Jonah packed his belongings and went down to the harbour where he booked himself on a cargo boat bound for Spain. The little boat set sail on a calm sea, but it was not long before a great storm blew up around it. Lightning flashed, thunder crashed and huge waves threatened to fill the boat with water. The sailors were very frightened. They began to throw the cargo overboard to make the boat lighter but still it was in danger of sinking. The captain went to wake Jonah who was asleep below deck. 'Wake up, Jonah!' the captain shouted above the noise of the storm. 'Pray to your God for help so that we may be saved.'
'I cannot pray to God,' said Jonah. 'I am running away from him.'
The sailors realised that the storm had been sent by God to punish Jonah, who told them to throw him into the sea so that the storm would stop. But the sailors liked him and tried to get the boat back to shore. It was impossible. The storm was getting worse and worse. Knowing that they would all be drowned if they did nothing, the sailors now picked up Jonah and threw him into the sea.
Immediately, the storm stopped and the water became calm again. The boat sailed on and Jonah was left alone, swimming far from the shore.
It wasn't long before Jonah felt a movement in the water beneath him and saw the shadow of a huge fish. The fish opened its mouth and sucked him inside, swallowing him in one gulp. Jonah found himself inside the stomach of the big fish. It was dark, wet and echoey. Jonah was very frightened and he prayed to God for help.
He had nearly given up hope when he felt himself being sucked out of the big fish's stomach, before being spat out on to soft, warm sand. As he stood up, he heard God's voice again telling him to go to Nineveh. This time Jonah set off at once to make the long journey across the desert to the foreign city.

Suggestion(s) for support
Because all parts of this activity allow for a variety of responses, less able children should be able to choose ways of responding which are suitable for them. They may prefer to present their experiences in a cartoon format rather than writing a narrative account.

Assessment opportunities
Asking the children about what happened in the Jonah story some time after this activity will indicate to what extent they have retained its outline and details. Reading the children's responses to the final exercise will provide evidence of their ability to identify the relevant experience in their own lives.

Opportunities for IT
Tell the groups that they are going to combine their efforts to create their own illustrated version of the story of Jonah, using a desktop publishing package. Set up a simple master page in advance, giving the paper sizes, working area and some styles for the fonts and sizes so that there is a consistency about the final book. The children can then work in small groups to illustrate their page and add the text to the story. If the children are using a desktop package they can easily position the text anywhere on the page, leaving space for the illustrations to be added. These can be included directly from an art or drawing package, possibly using suitable clip art to assist, or scanned from the children's own line drawings.

An alternative approach, or extension of the original idea, would be to make a talking book using multimedia authoring software (see 'Opportunities for IT', page 36).

Display ideas
A selection of the material prepared by the groups in the first part of the activity can be displayed under a heading such as 'Why did Jonah disobey God?' The written accounts and cartoon versions of the children's own experiences can be displayed nearby under a heading such as 'When we were told to…'

Reference to photocopiable sheet
Photocopiable page 131 provides a simple retelling of the story of Jonah up to the time when he was spat out by the fish. This is for use by the teacher in the initial retelling and by the children when working in their groups to remind them of the details of the story.

WHAT WORDS COULD BE USED TO GUIDE A PARTICULAR GROUP OF PEOPLE?

To understand the role of key words in binding a group together. To understand the importance of the Shema for Jews.

Guidance. Community.

†† *Groups of up to six followed by whole class and ending with individual/paired work.*

🕐 *Group work 30 minutes; whole class 15 minutes; individual/paired work as appropriate.*

Key background information

Mezuzah (the word literally means 'doorpost', plural 'mezuzot') is the title given to the small scroll within a case which is fixed at eye-level to the right-hand doorpost of a Jewish house, and other Jewish buildings too. Many Jews will also place a mezuzah on the right doorpost of all doors in the home, except for the toilet and bathroom. Upon entering and leaving their house, some Jews will touch the mezuzah and then lightly kiss their fingers. Matching sets of mezuzot are sometimes given as wedding presents.

Mezuzah cases are made in all kinds of material – including metal, clay, wood and plastic – and will usually have the Hebrew letter 'shin' (which resembles a capital 'W') on the front, the first sound of the word 'Shaddai' meaning 'Almighty'.

The handwritten scroll contains part of the Jewish prayer called the *Shema* (pronounced 'sh'mah'), which begins, 'Hear O Israel: the Lord our God, the Lord is One, and you shall love the Lord your God with all your heart, and with all your soul, and with all your might' (from the Jewish Torah, Deuteronomy, chapter 6, verse 4). The first word, 'hear', is *shema* in Hebrew. The Shema expresses central convictions of Judaism: that there is one God who should be placed before everything else.

As the idea of the mezuzah scroll being handled may not be acceptable to some Jews, it is recommended that the mezuzah case only is used in the classroom.

This activity epitomises the two attainment targets identified by the SCAA in their model syllabuses for religious education (see Introduction, page 8): 'learning about religion' and 'learning from religion'. In encouraging children to identify principles which should govern people's lives, it might also contribute to their moral and social development.

Preparation

Make copies of photocopiable page 132, one per group. Obtain a mezuzah case (see 'Useful books and resources', page 109) and become familiar with its design and purpose.

Resources needed

Mezuzah case; materials with which to make containers, such as margarine or ice-cream tubs with lids; kitchen rolls; foil; coloured paper; scissors; adhesive; photocopiable page 132; writing and drawing materials.

What to do

Divide the class into groups of a maximum of six. Give each group a copy of photocopiable page 132 and explain that their task is to complete the sentences so that they end up with four statements which express what everyone in their group believes. You may need to give some examples to clarify the task. For instance,

▲ Children should try to… work hard, be kind;

▲ Teachers should try to… listen to children, be fair;

▲ Parents should try to… spend time with their children, be kind to their children;

▲ Everybody should try to… smile at other people, look after the world.

Set a time limit for this task, after which give each group the opportunity to read their statements out to the whole class.

Next, ask the children to imagine that their group's statements (those written in the boxes) have been adopted by the whole class, who have agreed that abiding by the statements would make their world a better place in which to live. They must now write down in the final box on their photocopiable sheet as many ways as possible through which the class can be constantly reminded of what the statements say about how they should try to live their lives. Some examples could be given to clarify what is required. For example, the words could be written on the classroom wall,

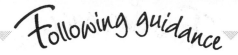

they could be recited at register time, all children could learn them by heart. Set a time limit for this new task after which the children can, once again, tell the whole class their ideas.

Tell the children that you are going to show them something which is special to Jewish people because it contains important words which remind them what they believe and how they should live their lives. Show the children a mezuzah case and talk about what it is and how it is used (see 'Key background information').

Finally, individually or in pairs, ask the children to design and make a special container for their statements. They should pay particular attention to:
▲ the design on the outside of their container;
▲ where the container is going to be placed;
▲ how people might treat the container;
▲ the way in which the statements are presented (for example, the use of decorated script).

Suggestion(s) for extension
Children who require extension work can be asked to find out more about the Shema, for instance where else the words might be placed, where the words can be found in the Torah/Christian Old Testament, and so on.

Suggestion(s) for support
Children who find the activity difficult could work together in a group supported by an adult helper. The adult could offer examples in order to encourage the children in their thinking.

Assessment opportunities
Listening to the group discussions during the first part of the activity will provide evidence of the extent to which they understand that certain words can be particularly relevant and emotive to a specific group. Children who carried out the extension activity could be asked to explain the importance of the Shema in order for you to see to what extent they have grasped its value for Jews.

Opportunities for IT
The children could write their statements using a word processor. They can then select suitable fonts in different sizes to create a version of their statement to fit inside their case. Other versions of the class statement can be printed out in large font sizes to make a display for the classroom wall.

The children could use a drawing or simple Computer Aided Design (CAD) package to draw the design for the statement container. They could also use an encyclopaedia CD-ROM or Nelson *Media Aspects of Religion* CD-ROM to find further information about the Shema and its importance for Jews.

Display ideas
Under a main heading such as 'Special words can guide a group', a display area could be divided into two parts. One part, with the heading 'The words of the Shema guide Jews' could feature the words of the Shema, a mezuzah case and accompanying explanation, and any other information which those carrying out the extension activity have found. Under the heading 'We thought of special words which could guide people we know', you could feature some of the group statements, examples of special containers and a list of ideas about how the containers and the special words could be used.

Reference to photocopiable sheet
The first four sections of photocopiable page 132 are for use at the beginning of the main activity and provides spaces for each group to complete the statements about how different people should live their lives. The final section of the sheet can be used to record the group's suggestions about how their key statements could be remembered and incorporated into people's lives.

HOW DO CHRISTIANS FOLLOW JESUS' EXAMPLE?

To know a story concerning the life of Jesus. To understand that many Christians would follow Jesus' example in reacting to situations of inappropriate behaviour or injustice.

Anger. Sacrilege.

Whole class followed by paired work.

⏱ *Whole class 30 minutes; paired work 30 minutes.*

Key background information

Evidence that the well-known story of Jesus overturning the money-changers' tables was an important one for early Christians is provided by the fact that all four Gospel writers included it in their Gospel books. John (chapter 2, verses 13–18), however, placed the incident at the start of Jesus' public life, whereas Matthew, Mark and Luke placed it during Jesus' final visit to Jerusalem.

In Jesus' day, the Jewish temple (which was eventually destroyed by the Romans in 70 CE) dominated the city of Jerusalem. From its centre – the 'Holy of Holies' – radiated a series of areas or courts. In the outermost area, pilgrims could buy sacrificial animals and birds (which had to be unblemished) but had to make their purchases using special temple coinage: Roman coins depicting the emperor's head were considered idolatrous. Money-changers provided a service by exchanging Roman coins for temple money. Religious necessity, however, could easily turn into hard trading which left pilgrims out of pocket, and this part of the temple, which people also used as a short cut, could appear more like a market than a sacred area.

In Mark's version of the story (chapter 11, verses 11–18), Jesus viewed the temple scene late one evening and then returned the following day when he caused the incident culminating in the declaration, 'Does not scripture say, "My house shall be called a house of prayer for all the nations"? But you have made it a robbers' cave.'

Preparation

Become familiar with the story of Jesus and the money-changers (see 'Key background information').

Resources needed

Writing and drawing materials. For the extension activity – children's Bibles.

What to do

Ask the children to think of a time when they have felt very angry. How did they express this anger? Choose several children to talk about their particular incident. Draw a distinction between feeling angry about something which has happened to you personally which was not your fault, for example someone calling you names, and feeling angry about something which affects other people or places, such as seeing a display of children's work in school which someone has damaged deliberately. Encourage the children to think of further examples of both of these types of anger.

Explain that Christians remember a story from their Bible in which Jesus displayed anger because of what he saw happening in the temple in Jerusalem. Tell the story to the children. Ask them which sort of anger Jesus was expressing and then develop their understanding of the story by posing questions.

▲ Why didn't Jesus turn over the tables on his first visit to the temple?

▲ Why did Jesus turn over the tables rather than asking the people to stop what they were doing?

▲ What was the meaning of the words that Jesus spoke?

▲ What does the story tell Christians about Jesus?

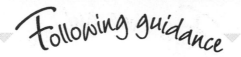

Working in pairs, ask the children to imagine a Christian today visiting a church building and finding something occurring there which makes him or her angry. Examples might include a large souvenir stall at the front, someone talking very loudly on a mobile phone, children playing with a ball. Together, they should identify the situation and then discuss in what way the person might react. Ask the children to record their ideas in text and/or pictures.

Suggestion(s) for extension
Ask children to compare two versions of the story by reading the accounts in Mark's and John's Gospels.

Suggestion(s) for support
Children could be given an imaginary situation rather than thinking of one themselves. For instance, a Christian walked into a church building to find a jumble sale taking place in the area where people met to worship; two people were arguing about who was going to buy a coat that one of them was holding.

Assessment opportunities
To find out whether the children have retained the story, ask them to recall the outline sometime after the activity has taken place. Through listening to the discussions between pairs and looking at their written or pictorial work it will be possible to assess to what extent the children have understood that Christians try to follow Jesus' example.

Assembly ideas
As part of an assembly focusing on a theme such as 'Feelings' or 'Stories from the Bible', the story of Jesus and the money-changers could be told or illustrated using a series of tableaux or freeze-frames depicting key scenes, characters and emotions. Several of the children's own modern-day situations could be described or acted out. You may like to end the assembly with a reflection such as, 'And now, in a moment of quiet, let us think about times when we feel angry. Could it be that we are too often angry because of something that happens to us and not angry often enough because of what we see happening to other people or places?'

WHERE DO SIKHS TURN FOR GUIDANCE IN CHOOSING NAMES?

To know that Sikhs consult their holy book in choosing a child's name. To encourage an interest in naming customs and the origin of names.

Guidance. Tradition.

†† *Whole class followed by individual work.*
🕐 *Whole class 20 minutes; individual work 30 minutes.*

Key background information
The importance of giving names to people and things is deeply embedded in human culture. Naming ceremonies often assume religious significance.

Sikhs look back historically to ten human Gurus (spiritual teachers), the last of whom stated that there would be no more human Gurus. Instead, the holy book, which included a collection of the teachings of the Gurus written in the Punjabi language, would be the Sikh community's Guru. Thus, the *Guru Granth Sahib* (the word *Granth* meaning 'book' and *Sahib* being a term of honour) is given the reverence due to a Guru and is looked to for guidance; its role within naming is therefore understandable.

In that Sikhs can use the same personal name for both boys and girls – Harjinder, for example, could be used for either sex – non-Sikh Westerners can sometimes become confused. It is the name which follows the personal name which is gender specific: *Singh* (meaning 'lion') is used by males and *Kaur* (meaning 'princess') by females. Thus, Harjinder Kaur would be female and Harjinder Singh male.

Preparation
Obtain a book or books giving information about the origins of names. If possible find some examples of illuminated letters. Gather together a selection of books and/or pictures about Sikhism (see 'Useful books and resources', page 109).

RELIGIOUS EDUCATION

So, for example, if the Punjabi letter is the 'm' sound, a name such as Mandeep might be chosen; if the 'r' sound, the name Ranjit might be selected.

Show the children some examples of illuminated letters. Ask the children to write their name in a decorative form using colour, shape and pattern. Underneath their name they should give an explanation as to why it was chosen, (children may need to consult their parents about this). The book of names can also be referred to, to find out further information about the name, such as its country of origin, its literal meaning, and so on.

Suggestion(s) for extension
Using the books and pictures you have obtained about Sikhism, ask the children to write an account of how Sikhs consult their holy book when choosing a name for a new-born baby.

Suggestion(s) for support
If children need help in researching and reading the information about their names try to arrange for an adult helper or support teacher to give them extra assistance.

Assessment opportunities
In order to establish whether the children have understood about the Sikh naming tradition, ask them to outline it during the final part of this activity or at a later stage.

Resources needed
Book or books about names; examples of illuminated letters; writing and drawing materials. For the extension activity – books and/or pictures about Sikhism.

What to do
Begin by asking the children if they know where their first name is derived from or why their first name was chosen. Talk about the different reasons for particular names being chosen, perhaps it was a family name, the name of a well-known or admired person, a name that cannot be shortened, a name with a particular meaning or symbolism, a name with religious connections.

Tell the children that most Sikhs follow tradition in choosing the name for a new-born baby. They use their holy book, the Guru Granth Sahib, to guide them in their choice. Explain that, as soon as possible after a baby is born, the family gather together at a gurdwara (Sikh place of worship) when other members of the community are already there for worship. The person reading the Guru Granth Sahib (the *Granthi*) opens the book at random and reads out the passage beginning at the top of the left-hand page. The Granthi then announces the first letter of the passage and the family chooses a name for their baby beginning with that letter.

Opportunities for IT
Show the children how to use an art package to create a decorative version of their name. They could do this either by using the drawing tools to draw the letters of their name, or using the text facility to type it in, possibly using a large font. The letters can then be decorated using the other tools of the art package. The decorative letter can be imported into a word-processing package and an explanation of why the name was chosen added. If each child in the class did this, the resulting packages could be published as a class book of names.

An alternative activity would be to create a database, initially of the class names, with a small number of fields which might be simply:

name	*Elizabeth*
sex	*female*
meaning	*oath of God*
reason	*grandmother's name*

If the database used has a 'tokens' field this could be used to categorise the reasons for the choice of name. This will limit the options but make the database more usable later on. The options might be:

RELIGIOUS
EDUCATION

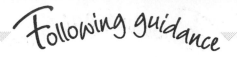

after a friend
after a member of the family
a family name
mother's preference
father's preference
holy name
religious reasons

The database could be extended to include every child in school. The children might have to do extra research to discover the meaning of some of the names.

Once the database has been completed the children could search for the most frequently occurring names, or reasons why names were chosen, presenting the results as a graph.

Display ideas

The children can mount and display their names and explanations under a title such as 'Why were we given our first names?' Adjacent to this, display the accounts written by those children carrying out the extension activity, together with any books or pictures used. This part of the display could be given a title such as 'How do Sikhs choose a name for a baby?'

HOW DOES THE BIBLE GIVE CHRISTIANS GUIDANCE?

To understand some of ways in which books of guidance offer support. To know that the Bible offers guidance to Christians.

Guidance. Holy book.

✝✝ *Small groups of about four followed by whole class and then individual work, ending with whole class.*

🕒 *Small group work 15 minutes; whole class 30 minutes; individual work 20 minutes; whole class 10 minutes.*

Key background information

While Christians would see certain key themes running through the writings of the Old and New Testaments, such as God searching for humankind and humankind searching for God, those who do not read or use the Bible regularly might find it a daunting 'book'. If of a certain age and belonging to a certain culture, they might have an inherited familiarity with certain biblical passages and stories which probably include, for example, the 23rd Psalm ('The Lord is my shepherd…'), Jesus' parables of the Prodigal Son (Luke, chapter 15) and the Good Samaritan (Luke, chapter 10), and Paul's words about faith, hope and charity/love (I Corinthians, chapter 13)

Teachers might wish to choose a biblical passage known to them to include in this activity. Otherwise, a passage such as Matthew, chapter 5 verses 43–44 (about loving your enemy) might be chosen. This passage was included by Matthew in a large collection of Jesus' teaching traditionally referred to as the 'Sermon on the Mount' (Matthew, chapters 5–7). For many today, Nelson Mandela, the South African President who spent 27 years in prison, has come to personify the spirit of this passage.

Preparation

Choose a passage from the Bible which can be used (see 'Key background information'). Make copies of photocopiable page 133 for children carrying out the extension activity.

Resources needed

Bible; writing and drawing materials. For the extension activity – children's Bibles; photocopiable page 133.

What to do

Divide the children into groups of about four. Ask each group to make a list of helpful things that could be included in a booklet which would be given to a new child to help her settle into the school. Offer several examples, such as her class timetable, a map of the school, names of teachers. Give the children a time limit for the completion of this task.

Bring the groups together and make a class list using ideas from each group. Discuss how a booklet containing these things would help the new child. She would know her way round the school, she would feel more secure, she would understand what was happening. Talk about how long the new child would need to use the booklet.

Ask the children to identify a book which they themselves use for guidance and then to write about it. They should include the following:
▲ the title of the book;
▲ its nature (what it is about);
▲ how often they use it;
▲ what would happen if it were lost.
Children can also include a drawing of the book.

Finally, explain that some people use a book to help them with the whole of their lives. Show the children a copy of the Bible and explain that many Christians refer to the Bible regularly for help and guidance. Read your chosen passage from the Bible and discuss in what ways it might help and guide a Christian who read it (see 'Key background information'). Take notes of the main ideas provided by the children.

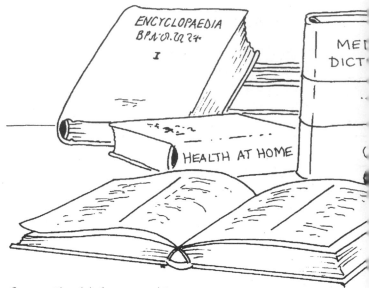

Suggestion(s) for extension
Give children a Bible and a copy of photocopiable page 133. Using the references listed they should find the relevant Bible passage and then complete the sheet by suggesting how the passages might offer guidance to Christians.

Suggestion(s) for support
Some children may need help in identifying books which they use for guidance. Examples could be offered from school life such as a dictionary, or home life, for instance a computer instruction manual.

Assessment opportunities
Both the results of the initial group work and the completed written task will provide evidence of the extent to which the children understand that a variety of books, including those important within individual religions, offer guidance to people during the course of their lives.

Display ideas
Ask the children to make a collection of the books that they use for guidance. Display these, together with their written accounts (some illustrated), under a heading such as 'Books we use for guidance'. A Bible could be displayed open at the

passage discussed by the whole class and children's ideas raised during the discussion could be displayed around it. The photocopiable sheets completed by those children who carried out the extension activity could be displayed alongside Bibles open at the relevant passages. A heading for this part of the display could be 'The Bible offers Christians guidance'.

Reference to photocopiable sheet

Photocopiable page 133 gives those children carrying out the extension activity a series of biblical passages which should be looked up in the Bible and read. The children then write about how these passages might offer guidance to Christians today.

WHAT ARE THE FIVE PILLARS OF ISLAM?

To know what the Five Pillars of Islam are. To understand how rules and duties can guide a community.

Duty. Community.

†† *Group work followed by whole class and then individual work.*

🕐 *Group work 15 minutes; whole class minimum of 30 minutes; individual work 20 minutes.*

Key background information

The description of the five basic duties of a Muslim as 'pillars' is a metaphor. In the same way as pillars strengthen and support a building, so the Five Pillars support and strengthen not only the individual Muslim but also the whole Muslim community (*ummah* in Arabic).

The Five Pillars:

▲ The statement of belief which crystalises what it means to be a Muslim is known as the *shahadah*. It is because Muhammad (*c*.570–632 CE) is believed to have been the (final) Messenger of God, rather than an object of worship, that the title 'Muhammadanism' should never be used. In becoming a Muslim, a person recites the statement of belief in the presence of Muslim witnesses.

▲ A Muslim may pray at any time, of course, but *salah* is the obligation to pray at five set times daily. These times will differ slightly during the year and a Muslim might refer to a chart to establish when they are. The bodily movements include kneeling with the forehead placed on the ground in front. This expresses the servant status of the human being in relation to *Allah* (God). Set prayer will be performed on clean ground – on a carpet in a mosque, or perhaps on a prayer-mat away from the mosque.

▲ Each year, Muslims are supposed to give a fixed proportion (one fortieth) of their savings for endeavours such as helping the poor. In this way, they believe, their wealth is 'made pure' (the meaning of the word *zakah*).

▲ Even Muslims who do not regularly pray five times daily will fast (*sawm*), refraining from water and food, during *Ramadan*. This is a month of increased devotion when Muslims try to live better lives and read the Qur'an regularly. The festival of *Id-ul-Fitr* immediately follows Ramadan.

▲ Muslims can make a pilgrimage to Makkah at any time, but *Hajj* must be made during the twelfth month.

Artefacts which could be used to enhance understanding include a plaque showing the statement of faith, a prayer-mat, a qiblah compass (used for finding the direction of the Ka'bah, faced by all Muslims during set prayer), a copy of the Qur'an, the white unsewn robes (*ihram*) worn by male Muslims during Hajj. Prayer beads will not be used during

set prayer by Muslims but might be used as an aid to prayer at other times.

Many educational video programmes on Islam will contain a section on the Five Pillars, for example *Islam through the Eyes of Muslim Children* (see 'Useful books and resources', page 109).

Preparation

Become familiar with information related to the Five Pillars and gather together pictures, video programmes and artefacts which can be used for explanatory information (see 'Useful books and resources', page 109). Make copies of photocopiable pages 134 and 135, enough for one per child.

Resources needed

Material to support information about the Five Pillars; photocopiable page 134; writing materials. For the assessment opportunities – photocopiable page 135.

What to do

Ask the children to imagine a scenario in which two schools are amalgamating. It is important that the people in the two schools come to feel that they belong to one community as quickly as possible. To help this to happen, the headteacher wants to find a number of things that everyone can do together. Give the children the task, in small groups, of thinking of at least three things that would create a strong sense of community. These could include wearing a uniform, meeting together as a whole school once a week, holding a school open day each year, and so on. Give a time limit for the groups to complete this task.

Bring the class back together and listen to each group's suggestions. Discuss which ones are most likely to be effective in creating a sense of community and shared purpose.

Next, tell the children that many communities have rules and duties which guide members, and that some of these are religious communities. Explain that Muslims have certain duties which they try to carry out and that, because these apply to Muslims everywhere, it helps them to feel that they are members of the worldwide Muslim community. These duties are called the 'Five Pillars' of Islam. Briefly explain what each of the pillars involves. If you have managed to obtain some relevant explanatory material refer to this when appropriate. Ask the children to make notes to help them with their work afterwards:

▲ the first pillar, shahadah in Arabic, is believing and saying the words, 'There is no god except Allah, Muhammad is the Messenger of Allah';

▲ the second pillar is salah, praying five times daily. These prayers are said using set words in Arabic, following a set sequence of bodily movements and facing in the direction of Makkah in Arabia. Preparation for prayer, including washing, is important;

▲ the third pillar, zakah, is giving some of your savings to be used for good purposes;

▲ the fourth pillar, sawm, is fasting during daylight hours of the month of Ramadan;

▲ the fifth pillar, Hajj, is making a pilgrimage to Makkah at least once in a lifetime if it can be afforded (see 'Why is the Ka'bah a special place for Muslims?', page 88).

Give each child a copy of photocopiable page 134 and ask them to complete it, writing down what each pillar represents, using their notes to help them. Their work can also include drawings.

Suggestion(s) for extension

Children requiring extension work can be asked to use books and other sources to find additional information about one or more of the Five Pillars.

Suggestion(s) for support

You may need to support the less able children by writing a translation of the Arabic words on each of the pillars on an enlarged sheet made from photocopiable page 134.

Assessment opportunities

Photocopiable page 135 provides an assessment task which will enable the teacher to establish how much knowledge the children have gained during this activity.

Opportunities for IT

Encourage the children to use an encyclopaedia CD-ROM or Nelson *Media Aspects of Religion* CD-ROM to research the Five Pillars of Islam.

Display ideas

Any books, pictures and artefacts used in the activity can be displayed, together with some of the completed photocopiable sheets. A large drawing of five pillars with the corresponding Arabic word written on each pillar could be used as a backdrop with a heading such as 'The Muslim community follows the Five Pillars for guidance' across the top (like a pediment on a building).

Reference to photocopiable sheets

Photocopiable page 134 provides space for the children to write information about each of the Five Pillars, referring to the notes made during the teacher exposition. Photocopiable page 135 is an assessment task aimed at ascertaining how much knowledge about the Five Pillars the children have gained.

HOW MIGHT THE FIVE PRECEPTS AFFECT A BUDDHIST'S LIFE?

To understand the role of promises in human experience. To understand how the Five Precepts might affect the life of a Buddhist.

Promise. Lifestyle.

†† *Whole class, individual work, returning to whole class.*

🕐 *Whole class 15 minutes; individual work 15 minutes; whole class 30 minutes.*

Key background information

It has sometimes been pointed out that, within Buddhism, there appear to be many numbered lists – such as the 'Four Sights' which Siddartha Gautama saw (see 'What sights could make us stop and think?', page 46), the 'Four Noble Truths' (the truths of existence basic to Buddhism) and the 'Noble Eightfold Path' (which outlines the 'middle way' that Buddhists should try to follow). A clear summary can be found in the CEM booklet *Teaching RE: Buddhism 5–11* (see 'Useful books and resources', page 109).

The Five Precepts are a list of promises or voluntary 'training principles' which many Buddhists adopt. They can each be expressed in a negative and a positive form:

▲ not to harm any living thing… to cultivate loving kindness and care for all living things;

▲ not to take what is not freely given… to cultivate generosity in all things;

▲ not to misuse the senses… to practise simplicity and contentment;

▲ not to use wrong speech… to practise truthful speech;

▲ not to take drugs or drink which cloud the mind… to practice awareness and mindfulness.

For many people today, the Dalai Lama, the exiled Buddhist Tibetan leader who was awarded the Nobel Peace Prize in 1989, is regarded as a personification of principles such as the Five Precepts.

RELIGIOUS EDUCATION

Following guidance

Preparation

Become familiar with the Five Precepts (see 'Key background information'). Make copies of photocopiable page 136. Make copies of photocopiable page 137 for those children carrying out the support activity.

Resources needed

Photocopiable page 136; writing materials. For the support activity – photocopiable page 137.

What to do

As a class, talk about promises the children have made in the past. These may include:

▲ personal promises made to friends, parents or teachers;

▲ public promises made in clubs or groups, for example at Brownies or Cubs.

Then lead the discussion into a broader consideration of promises, considering questions such as:

▲ Why do people make promises?

▲ Are promises always easy to keep?

▲ Are all promises good?

▲ How do you feel if you break a promise?

Explain to the children that some people make promises to guide them in their lives and that one example of this is the Five Precepts (or promises) which many Buddhists make. Give each child a copy of photocopiable page 136. Tell them to read through the sheet and then underline those instances which they think might be examples of a Buddhist person following a Precept. Having reviewed the parts which they have underlined, they should then list in the box what they think the Five Precepts might be.

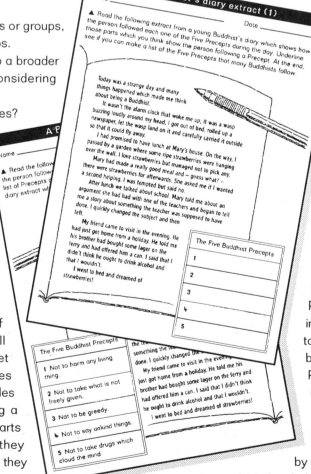

Bring the children together to check and compare their responses to the exercise and to discuss each of the Precepts in turn.

Suggestion(s) for extension

Ask children to make a list of ways in which each of the Five Precepts could be demonstrated in everyday life.

Suggestion(s) for support

Children who find the activity difficult should be given a copy of photocopiable page 137. This lists the Five Precepts in the box at the bottom of the sheet. The children should underline the relevant sections in the text and then write the number of the corresponding Precept next to it.

Assessment opportunities

The whole-class discussions at the beginning and end of this activity will provide broad evidence of the extent to which the children have understood the importance of promises and how the special promises, called the Five Precepts, might influence a Buddhist's approach to life.

Reference to photocopiable sheets

Photocopiable page 136 is for use in the main activity. With reference to the story the children write in the box what they think the Five Precepts which Buddhists adhere to might be. Photocopiable page 137, which lists the Five Precepts, is for use in the support activity. The children should underline and link by number those parts of the diary extract which they believe show a Precept in action.

64

Encountering special times

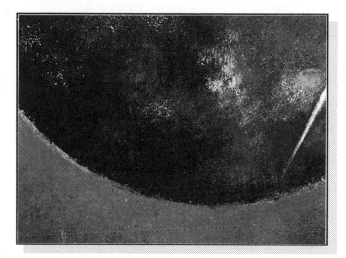

To be human, it could be said, is to celebrate. If there were no religion in the world, people would still feel the need to celebrate and to mark out special times as festivals. If there were no religious education in the curriculum, the passage of the primary school year would still be punctuated by special days and celebrations.

All but one of the activities in this chapter include material drawn from the celebratory life of the major religious traditions. Some of these activities, such as the one exploring the Hindu festival of Holi, do not move beyond an exploration of the nature and meaning of the religious material. But, given the twin dynamic of religious education ('learning about' and 'learning from' religion), other activities encourage children to reflect on fundamental aspects of their own experience. Thus, for example, an activity focusing on the Jewish festivals of Rosh Hashanah and Yom Kippur begins with the children being asked to think about the experience of forgiveness in their own lives.

For both cultural and religious reasons, the Easter and Christmas festivals are firmly established in primary school life. There has been a frequent concern, though, that classroom work focusing on them has lacked continuity and progression. As a safeguard, two activities are provided for each: a simpler one for Years 3 and 4, and a more demanding one (looking at the biblical basis of the Easter and Christmas stories) for Years 5 and 6.

HOW DO CHRISTIANS REMEMBER THE EVENTS OF HOLY WEEK?

To know the key events associated with Holy Week. To know some of the ways in which Christians today remember and relive these events.

Celebration. Faith.

†† *Group work followed by whole class and then individual work.*

🕐 *Group work 10 minutes; whole class 30 minutes; individual work 30 minutes.*

Key background information

The details of what happened during the week leading up to the first Easter Sunday are complex. The main sources of evidence – the Gospel writings of Matthew, Mark, Luke and John – were not written solely to provide historical accounts, exact in every detail. Moreover, the ways in which Christians today remember the events of Holy Week vary tremendously and are often deeply affected by the culture within which the celebrations are taking place. Teachers should guard against inadvertently giving the impression that Christianity is confined to what happens in Britain. There are general references below to what happens in other parts of the world: in the Philippines, church members process through the streets on Palm Sunday carrying plaited palm branches; in Mexico, some Christians dress completely in black during Holy Week as a sign of sadness; in Guatemala, statues of Jesus with money pinned to them are carried into churches on Easter Sunday, the money being used to carry out church work.

The Easter declaration 'Christ is risen! He is risen indeed!' referred to in the activity is part of the Easter Day service found within the Orthodox family of Christian churches.

Through its 'theatricality' and rich symbolism, Orthodox worship can be a useful resource for the classroom.

Teachers often find that teaching about Easter is far more difficult than teaching about Christmas. This is probably because Easter is rooted in events which are not 'neutral', but which are bound up in Christian belief and faith. The teacher's role, however, is not to 'teach the faith' but, rather, to present accurate and interesting information about Easter including what Christians believe was taking place in these events and how they express this in their lives today.

Preparation

Make copies of photocopiable page 138, one for each child. Obtain artefacts and pictures which can supplement the information about Holy Week, for instance a palm cross, a crucifix, a picture of a Holy Week procession (see 'Useful books and resources', page 109).

Resources needed

Photocopiable page 138; artefacts and pictures as appropriate; A3 paper; writing and drawing materials; scissors; adhesive.

What to do

Divide the children into groups and give each group a large sheet of paper. Explain that you want the children to recall as much information as they can about Easter and to write down this information on the sheet. (Each group should nominate a scribe to do this.) Set the children a time limit for this task.

Bring the groups together and ask each group to report back to the rest of the class, using their completed sheets of paper as a guide.

the Last Supper, it is said that Jesus washed the feet of his disciples to symbolise that greatness lies in serving others.

▲ *Good Friday* remembers Jesus' death by crucifixion at a place called Golgotha (Calvary) outside the city walls, followed by his burial in a borrowed rock tomb. For Christians, this is the most solemn day of the year and many churches remove or cover up ornaments and do not display flowers. In some parts of the world, people dress in black.

▲ *Easter Sunday* remembers the time when 'on the third day' some of Jesus' women followers discovered that the tomb in which Jesus had been buried was empty. They met Jesus again. Others soon had a similar meeting. For Christians, this is the most joyous day of the year. In some Christian groups, people gather in their darkened church late on Saturday evening. At midnight, the lights are all put on and people cry out 'Christ is Risen!' Others reply, 'He is risen indeed!' In some countries, people carry a statue of Jesus into their churches.

Give a copy of photocopiable page 138 to each child. Explain that the task is to cut out the pieces of information and then to paste them on to a separate sheet of paper in the correct order. When they have finished ask the children to draw an illustration for each special day of Holy Week, using a separate sheet of paper.

Next, expand on the children's knowledge by explaining that Easter is the most important time of the year for Christians. It celebrates the last week of Jesus' life when, they believe, he died and then came back to life and visited his followers. Tell the children that the week leading up to Easter Sunday is called 'Holy Week' and that, during it, Christians remember events connected with Jesus and his followers. Work through the events of the week, explaining the key days and supplying the following information supplemented as appropriate:

▲ *Palm Sunday* remembers the day when Jesus rode into Jerusalem on a donkey and crowds of people greeted him by spreading palm branches in his path. Many Christians today attend special Palm Sunday services. In some Christian groups, worshippers are each given a cross made from dried palm leaves which they take home afterwards. There are processions in many parts of the world.

▲ *Maundy Thursday* remembers the Last Supper which Jesus shared in Jerusalem with his 12 closest followers (disciples), his time of prayer in the Garden of Gethsemane outside the city, and his arrest by temple police as the result of betrayal by Judas Iscariot, one of the Twelve. There are many traditions associated with Maundy Thursday. In Britain, the giving of 'Maundy money' by the reigning monarch is an ancient tradition. In some Christian groups, there is the public washing of feet during a special service: in one account of

Suggestion(s) for extension

Those children who require extension work could either:

▲ produce an illustrated account of what happened during Holy Week and how Christians remember it; or

▲ imagine that they were somebody visiting Jerusalem during Holy Week and write a diary account of that time.

Suggestion(s) for support

Some children may need adult support when trying to match the separate pieces of information which they have cut out of photocopiable page 138.

They may find it helpful if you number the different sections relating to each of the four days with a corresponding number.

Assessment opportunities

The accuracy with which children are able to link together the statements on the photocopiable sheet will show to what extent they have learned the key events associated with Holy Week and some of the ways in which they are marked by Christians. The photocopiable sheet could also be used at a later date in order to establish the extent to which this knowledge has been retained.

What happened in Holy Week

Assembly ideas

As part of an assembly focusing on a theme such as 'Easter' or 'The life of Jesus', three narrators could talk about Holy Week. The first narrator announcing the day, the second outlining what happened at the first Easter, and the third describing some of the things that Christians do today. At appropriate points, other children could use mime or drama, create a tableau of a scene or show pictures or artefacts relating to the different events. The assembly could finish with a reflection such as, 'And now, in a moment of quiet, let us reflect upon what Christians experience each year at Easter – sadness suddenly changing into joy. Let us hope that, in our own lives, sadness will always turn to joy.'

Reference to photocopiable sheet

Twelve separate pieces of information relating to Holy Week are provided on photocopiable page 138. Children are required to cut out the statements on the sheet and connect the pieces of information together, putting the events in their correct chronological order.

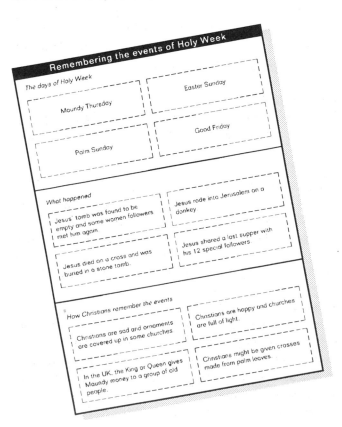

WHY IS LIGHT USED AS A SYMBOL AT CHRISTMAS?

To understand why light is used as a symbol at Christmas. To know how Christians might interpret the symbolism of a Christingle.

Symbolism. Celebration.

†† *Individual followed by whole class work, returning to individual work.*

🕐 *Individual work 10 minutes; whole class work 20 minutes; individual work 20–30 minutes.*

Key background information

Learning that people express ideas, values and beliefs in a wide variety of ways is fundamental to work in religious education. Exploring symbolism is therefore significant, though it must be remembered that symbols – unlike 'signs' – are fluid and their layers of meaning can never be fully exhausted. It is for this reason that, in this activity, the symbolism of a *Christingle* for a Christian is given with the awareness that some Christians might see other or further symbolic value, and the children themselves are given the opportunity to suggest further meanings.

Light is a universal symbol. Its use as a symbol, to represent such ideas as truth, knowledge, freedom and victory, has not been confined to one culture or time. The description of Jesus as 'Light of the World' belongs to the first years of Christianity. In John's Gospel (chapter 8, verse 12), Jesus himself declares, 'I am the light of the world. No follower of mine shall wander in the dark; he shall have the light of life.'

The use of the Christingle (Christ-light) originated in northern Germany. Many British churches now hold a Christingle service in which children are each given a

Christingle, often in exchange for money or a gift to be given to the needy. Similar symbolism can also be seen in the Swedish Saint Lucia festivities – in the use of lighted candles, a red sash, white clothing, a crown and evergreens, for example.

Preparation
Make a Christingle (see photocopiable page 139). Make copies of photocopiable page 139, one per child. Make copies of photocopiable page 140 for those children carrying out the extension activity.

Resources needed
A Christingle; photocopiable page 139; writing materials. For the extension activity – photocopiable page 140.

What to do
Give each of the children a blank piece of paper. Tell them to write the words 'Light at Christmas' in the middle and then, around the outside, to write the different ways that light is used at Christmas (such as Christmas tree lights, Advent candles, rows of electric 'candles' on wooden stands, street decorations) with possible reasons for their use (to make the house look special, to make people feel happy, to show that it is a special time, to remind people of Jesus). When they have finished, bring the children together and compile a

list of examples and reasons. Explain that light is used all over the world to help people express what they feel and believe and that when something is used like this it is called a 'symbol'.

Tell the children that some Christian groups go to church at Christmas time to attend a special service in which they think about Jesus' birth. They may sometimes be given something which symbolises their beliefs about Jesus. Show a lighted Christingle and point out its different features, explaining what each might symbolise to a Christian:
▲ the orange – the world;
▲ the red ribbon round the orange – the blood which Jesus shed at his death;
▲ the four cocktail sticks – the four corners of the world (or the four seasons);
▲ the fruit on the cocktail sticks – the fruits of the earth.

Then point to the lighted candle and explain that for Christians this might be a symbol which represents Jesus bringing light to the world. Discuss any other symbolism that the children can see in the features of a Christingle.

Finally, give each child a copy of photocopiable page 139, and ask them to label and explain the symbolism of the different parts of the Christingle. They should then write a couple of sentences about what they think Christians mean when they say that Jesus brings light to the world.

Suggestion(s) for extension
As an additional activity, give those children requiring extension work a copy of photocopiable page 140. Ask them to read about the festival of Saint Lucia, and then to write about the symbolism of the various features. (For instance, red sash – Jesus' blood; crown – Jesus as king (the crown of thorns); evergreen leaves – Jesus living on; lighted candles – Jesus bringing light to the world.)

Suggestion(s) for support
Any children who experience difficulties with the activity may find it easier just to complete the first part of photocopiable page 139.

Assessment opportunities
The first part of the main activity and the discussions which follow will indicate whether the concept of light as a symbol has been understood. Completed photocopiable page 139 will demonstrate to what extent the children have learned how Christians might interpret the symbolism of a Christingle.

Opportunities for IT
Allow the children to use an art or drawing package to make their own Christingle picture. They could also add labels to the picture to explain the symbolism of the various parts of the Christingle. Using a word processor the children can write their own interpretation of what they think is meant by the expression 'Jesus brings light to the world'.

Assembly ideas

As part of an assembly focusing on a theme such as 'Christmas' or 'Light', a variety of ways in which light is used as a symbol at Christmas, including the Christingle and Saint Lucia customs, could be shown and explained. You may like to end the assembly with a reflection such as, 'And now, in a moment of quiet, let us think about the use of light at Christmas and what the symbol of light means to each one of us at Christmas time.'

Reference to photocopiable sheets

Photocopiable page 139 provides a drawing of a Christingle for the children to label and explain. The second part of the sheet is more demanding and requires the children to explain the symbolism by describing what is meant when Christians say that Jesus brings light to the world. Photocopiable page 140 is for use in the extension activity. It gives a brief description of the Swedish Saint Lucia customs which children carrying out the activity should read in order to detect what symbolism is being used.

WHAT HAPPENED ON THE FIRST EASTER SUNDAY MORNING?

To compare and contrast material from different sources. To consider and raise questions about the different Christian accounts of what happened on the first Easter Sunday morning.

Fact. Truth.

✝✝ *Whole class followed by groups of four, returning to whole class.*

🕐 *Whole class 20 minutes; small groups 40 minutes; whole class 20–30 minutes.*

Key background information

That Christianity is based on the Easter experience of the first Christians is certain, but the details of what actually happened are harder to establish.

In using material from the Gospel writings, three things must be borne in mind. Firstly, though they come first in the New Testament list, they were not the first 'books' to have been written. The earliest writings are a series of letters written by (Saint) Paul to individuals and groups of Christians. Indeed, the earliest account of the resurrection and appearance of Jesus to his followers is found in one of these letters (Paul's First Letter to the Corinthians, chapter 15, verses 1–8). Secondly, the Gospels were written some time after the events and experiences that they describe. Many think that Mark's Gospel was the first Gospel to have been written in about 65 CE (approximately 35 years after Jesus'

RELIGIOUS EDUCATION

crucifixion) and that Luke and Matthew some years later used Mark's Gospel as a major source for their own. Thirdly, the Gospel writers were not writing 'neutral' accounts: they had strong beliefs about the significance of the events and wanted others to share them. It is sometimes said that they were proclaiming rather than describing.

A number of reasons can be suggested for the differences in their accounts of the first Easter Sunday morning, for example the writers were using different sources and wanted to make different points.

Preparation
Make copies of photocopiable page 141, enough for one per child. Become familiar with the Holy Week 'storyline'. Obtain either enough children's Bibles for at least one copy per group or make copies of the different Gospel writers' versions of the events of that week.

Resources needed
Photocopiable page 141; children's Bibles or extracts; writing materials.

What to do
Begin by briefly recalling the events of Holy Week (see 'How do Christians remember the events of Holy Week?', page 66) so that the children are able to grasp the 'storyline'.
▲ Jesus, at about the age of 30, was in Jerusalem.
▲ Jerusalem was packed with Jewish pilgrims because it was the Passover festival.
▲ The Romans were anxious about the possibility of trouble.
▲ The Jewish leaders were deeply angered by Jesus because of some of the things he was saying and wanted him out of the way.

▲ Jesus and his close followers stayed in a village outside Jerusalem but spent each day in the city.
▲ On the Thursday evening, Jesus had a last supper with his 12 special disciples.
▲ After the supper Jesus went with his three closest disciples to the garden of Gethsemane to pray.
▲ Jesus was betrayed (Judas Iscariot told the temple police that Jesus could be arrested in the garden – away from crowds and a possible riot).
▲ Overnight, Jesus was tried by the Jewish leaders and then by the Roman governor, Pontius Pilate, who condemned him to death by crucifixion.
▲ On the Friday, Jesus was forced to carry the main part of the cross through the streets to the execution place outside Jerusalem (Golgotha or Calvary).
▲ Jesus was crucified, died and was buried in a rock tomb.
▲ Because the Sabbath was about to start, his closest followers (all Jewish) could not visit the tomb to anoint Jesus' body (that is, perform customary rituals such as placing sweet-smelling spices on the body) but had to wait till the Sabbath was over.
▲ Some of his followers went to the tomb first thing on the Sunday morning in order to anoint the body.

Next, explain to the children that working in groups of four, they will be researching what was said to have happened when some of Jesus' followers returned to the tomb early on the Sunday morning. Tell the children that there are four different accounts of what happened. These were written by Christians called Matthew, Mark, Luke and John. Explain that the groups should carefully read each of the four accounts, answering the questions on the photocopiable sheet in the relevant column. Set a time limit for this task.

RELIGIOUS EDUCATION

At the end of the specified time, bring the groups together and, as a class, discuss what the groups found in each account. Ask questions in order to encourage the children to think about the significance of what they have been reading.

▲ What things are common to all four accounts?

▲ What are the major differences between the accounts?

▲ Does it matter that there are differences between the accounts?

▲ Why are there differences?

Encourage the children to raise questions of their own.

Suggestion(s) for extension

The more able children could refer to Luke's Gospel in order to see what this writer said happened on the road to Emmaus some time after the discovery of the empty tomb (Luke, chapter 24, verses 10–32).

Suggestion(s) for support

Because the language used in the four Gospel accounts will be in part unfamiliar, children who are less confident with reading might be placed in groups with more competent readers.

Assessment opportunities

The degree of accuracy with which children complete photocopiable page 141 will indicate to what extent the children are able to compare and contrast material from different sources. The class discussion at the end of the activity will demonstrate the children's abilities to consider and raise questions about the accounts they have been looking at.

Opportunities for IT

Older or more able children could work from texts of the four gospels taken from a CD-ROM. If the texts are loaded into a word processor beforehand the children could then re-order the texts to locate and group the same parts of the story from the different gospels. Ensure that the children know how to mark and move text around the screen using 'cut and paste' or 'drag and drop' commands. If the children use a desktop publishing package they can write their own commentary about the differences in a separate frame:

Matthew	text from gospels grouped by the same part of the story	children's written commentary about how the versions agree or disagree
Mark		

The children could also learn how to use the search commands to look for important key words in the story.

Reference to photocopiable sheet

Photocopiable page 141 gives the references for the four different Gospel accounts of the Easter story. The children are required to answer a series of questions, noting down details in the relevant columns.

Four early Christians – Matthew, Mark, Luke and John – each wrote an account of what happened when, at first light on the Sunday morning, people went to the tomb in which Jesus' body had been placed. Look at each of these accounts in turn and, using the questions below as a guide, write a summary of what each writer wrote. If you have time, compare the four summaries, looking for similarities and differences.

	Mark, chapter 16, verses 1–8	Matthew, chapter 28, verses 1–10	Luke, chapter 24, verses 1–11	John, chapter 20, verses 1–18
▲ Who went to the tomb?				
▲ When did they go?				
▲ Why did they go?				
▲ What were they thinking about?				
▲ What did they see and hear at the tomb?				
▲ What did they do?				

The first Easter Sunday morning

Name

Date

RELIGIOUS EDUCATION

WHAT ARE THE ORIGINS OF THE FAMILIAR CHRISTMAS STORY?

To understand that the traditional Christmas story derives from several sources. To compare and contrast material from different sources.

Source. Tradition.

†† *Paired work followed by whole class, returning to pairs.*

⏰ *Paired work 10 minutes; whole class 25 minutes; paired work 25 minutes.*

Key background information

The familiar 'Christmas story' derives from several sources: biblical accounts and later additions which have been made through the ages. This activity provides the opportunity for children to look carefully at the biblical sources of the story, while the extension activity includes an opportunity to identify additional details.

Of the four Gospel writers whose writings begin the Christian New Testament, only Matthew and Luke chose to write about Jesus' birth. Mark and John, by contrast, began their 'good news' (what the word *gospel* means) with Jesus at the age of about 30.

Though both Christians, Luke and Matthew came from different backgrounds (Matthew's was Jewish, Luke's was not) and wrote with different emphases. Luke, for example, developed the theme of poverty in his Gospel. It is in his account that Jesus is born in a stable. Matthew developed the theme of kingship: it is in his Gospel that astrologers/magi visit Jesus (in a house) and bring gifts fit for a king.

Preparation

Make copies of photocopiable page 142, one for each pair. Obtain either a sufficient number of Bibles or copies of Matthew's and Luke's accounts, one per pair.

Resources needed

Photocopiable page 142; Bibles or Gospel accounts; writing materials.

What to do

Tell the children to work in pairs and to write brief notes listing the events that they remember happening in the Christmas story. Ask them to try to put the events in sequence. When they have finished, choose several pairs to read out their notes asking the rest of the class to listen and compare similarities and differences in what they have written. Discuss as a class possible reasons why some aspects of the story are the same and others are not. Perhaps some parts of the story are told every year in school, others are favourite parts of the story, some are scenes shown on Christmas cards, lapses in memory, and so on.

Explain that the beginnings of the Christmas story are to be found in two different accounts written by early Christians called Luke and Matthew. These accounts are to be found at the start of the Gospels (books) which they wrote and are included in the New Testament part of the Christian Bible.

RELIGIOUS EDUCATION

Ask children to read out the two versions of the Christmas story from Matthew (chapter 2, verses 1–15) and then Luke (chapter 2, verses 1–20). As a class, briefly discuss the major differences in content. For example:

▲ only Luke refers to shepherds;
▲ only Matthew refers to wise men/astrologers;
▲ only Luke refers to a stable;
▲ only Matthew refers to a star.

Tell the children to work in their pairs again, giving each pair a copy of photocopiable page 142 and either a copy of the Bible or the passages from Luke and Matthew. Explain that their task is to read the passages for themselves and then, using the photocopiable sheet, to note down those details of the story which were included only by Matthew, those only included by Luke and those which occur in both Gospels. When they have finished, they should join up with another pair and compare what they have written on their sheets.

Suggestion(s) for extension

The more able children could compare the two biblical accounts with the notes from the exercise carried out at the beginning of this activity. They could then see whether the Christmas story which children in the class remembered:

▲ combined material from Matthew and Luke, for example the wise men visiting Jesus in a stable;
▲ added extra details to the accounts found in Matthew and Luke, such as specifying that there were three wise men.

Suggestion(s) for support

Because the language used in Matthew's and Luke's accounts will be in part unfamiliar, some children may benefit from being paired with more confident readers.

Assessment opportunities

The information which the children record on the photocopiable sheets will demonstrate their ability to compare and contrast material from different sources.

Display ideas

Under a heading such as 'What are the origins of the familiar Christmas story?', two central panels could contain summaries of the main details found in each of Matthew's and Luke's accounts (utilising material from the photocopiable sheets). A variety of pictorial material could be displayed around the panels, such as Christmas cards, posters, postcards of Christmas stamps, children's drawings or paintings, reproductions of classic art. Where there is an obvious link between a picture and a detail in Matthew's or Luke's accounts, this could be highlighted by joining the two with a piece of ribbon.

Reference to photocopiable sheet

Photocopiable page 142 is divided into three sections. It requires the children to note down features of the Christmas story found uniquely in Matthew or Luke or found in both.

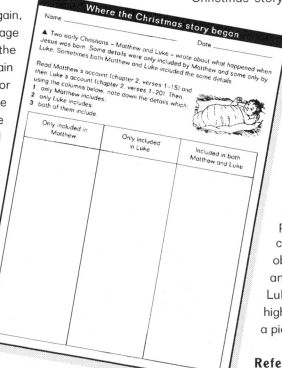

Where the Christmas story began

Name _____   Date _____

▲ Two early Christians – Matthew and Luke – wrote about what happened when Jesus was born. Some details were only included by Matthew and some only by Luke. Sometimes both Matthew and Luke included the same details.

Read Matthew's account (chapter 2, verses 1–15) and then Luke's account (chapter 2, verses 1–20). Then, using the columns below, note down the details which:
1 only Matthew includes;
2 only Luke includes;
3 both of them include.

Only included in Matthew	Only included in Luke	Included in both Matthew and Luke

WHEN DO JEWISH CHILDREN BECOME ADULT?

To understand the importance of Bar Mitzvah and Bat Mitzvah within the Jewish community. To know what several Jewish artefacts are and how they relate to Bar Mitzvah and Bat Mitzvah.

Coming of age. Ceremony.

†† *Whole class followed by individual work.*

⏰ *Whole class 25 minutes; individual work 20 minutes.*

Key background information

Among Jews there is great variety in practice, both within Britain and elsewhere in the world. Some Jews, for example, classify themselves as 'secular' or 'non-observant'; others as 'religious' or 'observant'. In Britain, those with a strong sense of religious identity will probably belong either to an 'Orthodox' or to a 'Reform' community.

Within Orthodox communities, the *Bar Mitzvah* takes place in the synagogue usually on the Sabbath following the boy's thirteenth birthday. Within a Reform Jewish community, however, it is likely that a Sabbath service will include both Bar Mitzvah and *Bat Mitzvah*. The Bat Mitzvah takes place for girls from 12 years old. In the ceremony both boy and girl wear a tallit (fringed prayer-shawl) and read out a passage from the Torah in Hebrew.

A Bar Mitzvah or Bat Mitzvah is a time of great social celebration, too, and there will be a party which will include family, friends, work associates and neighbours.

In Judaism, a mitzvah (plural 'mitzvot') is a commandment or religious duty. In becoming Bar Mitzvah (literally 'son of commandment', more colloquially 'man of duty'), then, a boy assumes religious adulthood with its obligations for following the mitzvot. So, too, a Bat (daughter) Mitzvah girl.

Leo Rosten's scholarly and humorous *The Joys of Yiddish* provides a mine of information about all things Jewish including Bar Mitzvah and mitzvot. Further information and teaching suggestions relating to the *tallit, yad* (literally 'hand', a pointer used for following text in the Torah) and *Torah scroll* can be found in *Religious Artefacts in the Classroom* by Jan Thompson and Paul Gateshill (see 'Useful books and resources', page 109).

Preparation

Obtain a miniature Torah scroll, yad and tallit together with pictures showing their use. Make copies of photocopiable page 143, one for each child.

Resources needed

Jewish artefacts; pictures; writing materials; photocopiable page 143.

What to do

Show the children the miniature Torah scroll, reminding them that it is a Jewish sacred text and should be treated with respect. Explain that the writing on the scroll is never touched by hand in case it gets marked and so, in order to follow the text, Jews who are reading from it use a pointer called a yad. Show the children a yad. Look carefully at the Hebrew script and tell the children that to mark the passage from childhood to adulthood all Jewish boys and many Jewish girls have to learn to read part of the Torah scroll in Hebrew. This special time is called Bar Mitzvah for a boy and Bat Mitzvah for a girl and takes place when a girl is 12 and a boy is 13.

RELIGIOUS EDUCATION

Explain to the children that not all Jewish groups celebrate Bar Mitzvah and Bat Mitzvah in the same way. For Jewish boys in Orthodox synagogues, for example:

▲ The ceremony will take place during the Sabbath service following his thirteenth birthday.

▲ At a point in the service, he will be called forward to the *bimah* (the raised platform from which readings are read) and will read out a passage from the Torah in Hebrew;

▲ He will wear a tallit (prayer-shawl) to show that he is now an adult.

▲ He will sit with the men in their section of the synagogue.

For a girl belonging to an Orthodox Jewish family, her Bat Mitzvah would usually take place on the Sunday nearest to her twelfth birthday; she would not wear a tallit and would not be expected to read from the Torah scroll. In a Reform synagogue, by contrast, a Bat Mitzvah is exactly the same as a Bar Mitzvah. Reform synagogues do not separate men and women, so there is no need to move to another section of the synagogue. If you have managed to obtain a tallit show this to the children or show them a picture of a Jew wearing one.

Give each child a copy of photocopiable page 143 and explain that their task is to write an account of what happens at a Jewish Bar Mitzvah and Bat Mitzvah. Their account should include reference to each of the three artefacts shown on the sheet.

Suggestion(s) for extension

After children have completed the above activity ask them to find out further information regarding the three different artefacts depicted on the sheet. Tell them to write what they find out on a separate sheet of paper.

Suggestion(s) for support

To assist them in completing their account of a Bar Mitzvah and Bat Mitzvah, some children may find it helpful to be given a number of key words, for example, 'synagogue', 'Sabbath', 'bimah', 'ceremony', 'Hebrew'.

Assessment opportunities

Photocopiable page 143 could be used as an assessment exercise by the whole class some time after the activity. The children could be asked to identify each of the artefacts and to state how it relates to Jewish Bar Mitzvah and Bat Mitzvah.

Opportunities for IT

Ask the children to use an encyclopaedia CD-ROM or Nelson *Media Aspects of Religion* CD-ROM to find out more about the customs and practices of the Bar/Bat Mitzvah.

Display ideas

Under a heading such as 'Bar Mitzvah and Bat Mitzvah is a special time for Jewish children', the artefacts, pictures and children's work can be displayed.

Reference to photocopiable sheet

Photocopiable page 143 has drawings of a Jewish scroll, yad, and tallit for the children to refer to when writing their account of what happens at a Bar Mitzvah or Bat Mitzvah at the bottom of the sheet. The sheet can also be used for assessment at a later date to see how much information the children have retained about a Jewish Bar Mitzvah and Bat Mitzvah. Those children carrying out the extension activity are asked to find out more about the three artefacts.

RELIGIOUS EDUCATION

WHAT DO JEWS DO AT ROSH HASHANAH AND YOM KIPPUR?

To reflect on aspects of experience related to seeking forgiveness. To understand the significance of Rosh Hashanah and Yom Kippur for Jews.

Forgiveness. Repentance.

†† *Friendship pairs followed by whole class and then individual work.*

🕐 *Friendship pairs 10 minutes; whole class 25 minutes; individual work 20 minutes.*

Key background information

Many beliefs, attitudes and customs are associated with the 'High Holy Days' of *Rosh Hashanah* and *Yom Kippur*. Ideally, the details referred to in this activity should be supplemented by other material such as video programmes, pictorial material, visitors and artefacts (such as a Jewish New Year card, a shofar and white kippah).

Rosh Hashanah is Jewish New Year (rosh meaning head, shanah meaning year, thus 'head of the year', the beginning of a new year) and occurs in late September or early October. It begins the ten 'Days of Penitence' which culminate in Yom Kippur, the Day (Yom in Hebrew) of Atonement, the holiest day of the Jewish year. Some link the use of white at Yom Kippur with the verse in Isaiah, chapter 1, verse 18 'even if your sins will be as red as scarlet they will become as white as snow'. The book of Jonah (see 'Why did Jonah change his mind?', page 52), which is read in the synagogue on Yom Kippur, has as its central theme God's willingness to forgive those who truly repent. The shofar, the curved ram's horn,

is blown three times on Rosh Hashanah. A long wailing note is the sign that Yom Kippur is over. It is suggested that the children work in friendship pairs at the beginning of this exercise. This is because the experiences being thought of may be of a personal nature. For the same reason, it is suggested that volunteers only be asked to share their experiences with the whole class.

Preparation

Make copies of photocopiable page 144, one for each child. Collect several Bibles and/or retellings of the Jonah story for use by those children carrying out the extension activity. Obtain related artefacts and other supporting material, if applicable.

Resources needed

Photocopiable page 144; artefacts and other supporting material, as appropriate; writing materials. For the extension activity – Bibles and/or Jonah story books.

What to do

Ask the children to work with a friend and to talk about a time when they have done something which they have felt sorry for afterwards and have wanted to be forgiven. They should talk about:
▲ why they felt sorry;
▲ why they wanted to be forgiven;
▲ whether they said sorry;
▲ how they felt afterwards.

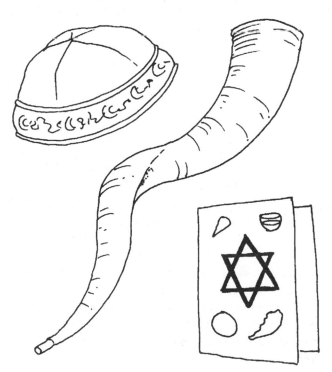

RELIGIOUS EDUCATION

When both partners have had the opportunity to talk, ask for several volunteers to share their experiences with the rest of the class. (You might like to begin this process by sharing an experience of your own.)

Next, explain that for Jews there is a particular time of year when they ask forgiveness from people to whom they have done wrong. This time begins with the festival of Rosh Hashanah and ends, ten days later, with the festival of Yom Kippur. Tell the children that Rosh Hashanah is a happy festival which marks the beginning of the Jewish New Year (see 'Key background information'). Jews eat special foods, wear new clothes and send each other New Year cards. Some Jews follow the custom of eating pieces of apple dipped in honey which symbolises the hope for a sweet (good) new year.

However, it is also the beginning of ten days when Jews remember the past year and try to put right things that have gone wrong. This period is an opportunity to ask people for forgiveness before the festival of Yom Kippur which ends the ten days. Yom Kippur (see 'Key background information'), when Jews ask God for forgiveness, is the most solemn day of the Jewish year. To show how sorry they feel, Jews fast, and spend as much time as possible praying in the synagogue and listening to readings from the Torah and other writings (including the book of Jonah). Many Jews will wear white on Yom Kippur. Men might wear a white *kippah* (head covering), for example. Yom Kippur ends with a *shofar*, a ram's horn, being blown.

Give each child a copy of photocopiable page 144. Explain that all the sentences have missing words which need to be filled in and three sentences need to be completed.

Suggestion(s) for extension

The more able children could be given the task of reading the story of Jonah (either the biblical book or a retelling of it) and deciding why Jews read this out in the synagogue on Yom Kippur.

Suggestion(s) for support

Some children may find it easier to complete the photocopiable sheet if they begin by filling in the missing words. They can then discuss the incomplete sentences with a teacher or support teacher before completing them.

Assessment opportunities

The quality of the paired discussions at the beginning of the activity will provide general evidence as to whether children are able to reflect on incidents in their lives which have required forgiveness, though individual children may show a particular sensitivity in working on such a task. The completed photocopiable sheet will indicate whether children have understood the significance of Rosh Hashanah and Yom Kippur for Jews.

Reference to photocopiable sheet

Photocopiable page 144 gives a number of statements about Rosh Hashanah and Yom Kippur. The children have to supply nine missing words and complete three sentences which will draw upon their understanding of these Jewish festivals.

Rosh Hashanah and Yom Kippur

Name _____   Date _____

▲ Referring to the list at the bottom of this sheet, fill in the missing words. When you complete sentences, think carefully about the reasons you are giving.

1 Rosh Hashanah is the Jewish _____ Year.

2 Some Jews eat pieces of apple dipped in _____ to show...

3 In the _____ days between Rosh Hashanah and Yom Kippur, Jews ask for _____ from those to whom they might have done wrong over the last year.

4 Yom Kippur is the most _____ day of the Jewish year.

5 On Yom Kippur, Jews go to the _____ to ask forgiveness of _____.

6 Many Jews wear _____ on Yom Kippur to show...

7 Jews fast on Yom Kippur because...

8 At the end of Yom Kippur, a ram's horn called a _____ is blown in the synagogue.

solemn   white   forgiveness   God   shofar   New   synagogue   ten   honey

Encountering special places

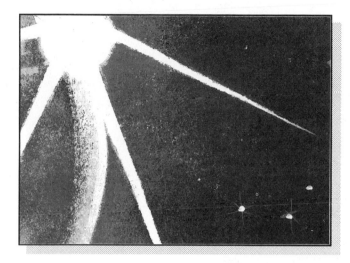

As individuals grow and develop, the number of places which they consider 'special' increases. They might be places of private significance associated with life-changing events or encounters with others, or they might be places associated with happiness or completeness in the past which are increasingly thought of with a kind of wistful longing.

All religious traditions have their special places, and it is important to understand their role and value for a particular community, though care must be taken not to overgeneralise. It must also be remembered that within many religious traditions there will be some who are deeply suspicious of an overemphasis on the physicality of the special place at the expense, they would say, of the 'inner' and most precious special place of all.

The activities in this chapter provide the opportunity to learn about special places associated with five of the principal religious traditions. In each case, care has been taken to move beyond the simple accumulation of technical or architectural detail to focus on an aspect of the special place which touches on important beliefs and values. Where appropriate, opportunities are provided for the children either to consolidate what they have learned or to apply insights to new situations. In one instance, a story is used as a context for the children to reflect on a place which is essentially memorable for them.

WHERE DO I REMEMBER BEING HAPPY?

To encourage reflection on the range of feelings associated with a place where a person has been happy. To express feelings using an appropriate medium.

Special place. Nostalgia.

†† *Whole class followed by small groups and then individual work.*

🕐 *Whole class 20 minutes; small groups 15 minutes; individual work as appropriate.*

Key background information

In this activity, it is that feeling of wistful longing, combining both delight and sadness, which people sometimes experience when they talk about past places (or times) where they were happy which is explored. The story of *Babylon* (by Jill Paton Walsh), used as a starting point, successfully captures this emotion, which takes on a religious aspect when the children talk about Babylon (and the song *By the waters of Babylon*, based on the psalm in which the ancient Jews, exiled in Babylon, looked back to their days in 'Zion', Jerusalem) and one of the boys then links Zion with Africa (as in Rastafarian belief).

Exploration of emotions connected with special places will not only promote self-understanding but will also provide a good base for an understanding of religious pilgrimage – an activity which, for the pilgrim, is usually a highly emotive event.

Preparation

Obtain a copy of *Babylon* (Beaver Books, 1985) and become familiar with the story. Obtain a recording of a piece of music which was composed in response to a particular place, for example 'Fingal's Cave' from the *Hebrides Overture* by Mendelssohn.

Resources needed

Babylon; piece of recorded music; writing and drawing materials; a range of musical instruments.

What to do

Gather the children together and read them the story of *Babylon*. Talk about the people's feelings in the story and explore these by asking questions.

▲ Why did Dulcie want to walk along the viaduct?

▲ Why did the children walk high and happy among the weeds flowering on the viaduct?

▲ Why did Dulcie say they were in Babylon?

▲ What made the boys think about Jamaica?

▲ Why did Dulcie feel sad?

▲ What made Dulcie cheer up?

Divide the children into small groups and ask each person within the group to talk about a place where they remember being happy. Encourage them to talk about their feelings as they speak about their memories.

When all the children have had an opportunity to speak, play the piece of music you have chosen, and explain that the composer wrote the music to express his feelings about a particular place where he had been and in order to remember that place.

Finally, ask the children to try to recapture their memories and express their feelings about their own special place through one of the following:

▲ writing a poem;

▲ using instruments to compose a piece of music, or writing the words of a song;

▲ writing a story;

▲ painting a picture.

Suggestion(s) for extension

Those children who find it easier to identify and explore feelings could be asked to choose a second medium in which to express their feelings and memories.

Suggestion(s) for support

Children who find it difficult to identify a special place may benefit from discussion with a support teacher or adult helper. If they still find it difficult to think of a place, ask them to choose one of the four suggested media and to express their own feelings about the viaduct in the story.

Assessment opportunities

While the children are working in groups, listening to them talking about their feelings when they remember a place where they were happy will give an indication of the extent to which they are able to reflect on such things. A child who is able to express feelings using an appropriate medium will be able to talk about her feelings and the reasons why a particular medium was chosen to express them.

Display ideas

Under a heading such as 'We thought about places where we had been happy and then expressed our feelings in a number of ways', display the children's work. A copy of *Babylon* could be placed on a table in front of the mounted work, together with the range of instruments which the children used when composing their music.

HOW CAN A CHURCH REVEAL WHAT CHRISTIANS THINK IS IMPORTANT?

To know some of the key features of a church building. To understand that what Christians believe to be important is reflected in a church building.

Special place. Design.

†† *Individual work and whole class during the church visit; whole class and paired work after the visit.*

🕑 *Church visit: individual work 30 minutes; whole class 30 minutes. Classroom: whole class 15 minutes; paired work 40 minutes.*

Key background information

The details of this activity are clearly going to be influenced by the type of church visited, but it takes as its premise that all church buildings, from the simplest Quaker meeting house to the most ornate Roman Catholic church, will 'make a statement' about the beliefs and values of the communities that use them.

In designing the worksheet to be used during the visit, the teacher will want to concentrate the children's attention on those features which can be thought about upon return to school. For example:

▲ a display of Sunday School work... evidence of the importance placed on learning about being a Christian;

▲ a stained glass window showing Jesus calling some disciples... evidence of the importance placed on following Jesus;

▲ the carved or embroidered letters 'IHS' (an anglicisation of the first three letters of the Greek word for 'Jesus')... evidence of the importance placed on Jesus;

▲ magazines and posters about missionary work... evidence of the importance placed on telling others about being a Christian;

▲ a font or a framed 'cradle roll'... evidence of the importance placed on welcoming new individuals into the Christian family.

Preparation

First make contact with the church to be visited. Arrange a preliminary visit, and agree the purposes of the visit with the contact person. Arrange for someone to talk to the children about the church building and clarify the purpose of the presentation. Design and photocopy a worksheet for use during the visit. Make copies of photocopiable page 145, one for each child, for use after the visit.

Resources needed

Person to speak with the children at the church; worksheet; photocopiable page 145; writing and drawing materials; loaded camera.

What to do

Take the children on a visit to a local church, reminding them that a church building is a special place for Christians and that they should behave appropriately. Give each child a copy of the worksheet which you have prepared for the church visit and explain that they will need to refer to the features of the church when completing the sheet (see 'Key background information'). Take photographs of key features as appropriate.

When the children have had sufficient time to complete their sheets, gather them together and explain that a member of the church community is going to talk to them about what happens in the church building and what the building means for him or her personally. Allow time for questions and answers after the presentation.

When everyone has returned to school, discuss what has been seen and heard during the visit. Explain to the children that you want them to consider what they heard and saw, and what it tells them about things to which Christians attach importance. Give each child a copy of photocopiable page 145. Tell them that they are going to complete this by responding to the different sections on the sheet, working in pairs. Demonstrate the task by discussing the first question as a whole class. As the pairs finish their sheets, they could go on to draw, paint or write about parts of the church which they found particularly interesting or significant.

Suggestion(s) for extension

Working as a group, the children could create a glossary of key terms related to a church building.

Suggestion(s) for support

During the first part of the church visit, adults could accompany the children in order to help them complete their worksheet. When completing the sections on photocopiable page 145, the children may need to be reminded of what they saw and heard, and may need help in drawing out the significance of their observations gained during their visit to the church.

Assessment opportunities

Using the glossary prepared by the children who carried out the extension activity, the whole class could be asked to supply definitions to key terms in order to establish the extent of the children's knowledge of the key features of a church building. If the children's responses reveal inadequate knowledge, they could be set a learning task followed by a test. The amount of evidence used in completing the photocopiable sheet will indicate the extent to which children have understood that what Christians believe to be important is reflected in a church building.

Opportunities for IT

Let the children use a word processor to write a glossary of the different parts of the church. A main list of terms could be drawn up by the class and children can research and define their allocated words. The glossary could also be formatted so that it forms part of a class display. The children may also like to create a pictorial glossary. This can be done using pictures taken from a selection of clip art in a drawing package.

The children could also use Framework software such as *My World 2* with the Places of Worship file to design their own church. They can then print the net and use it to make a 3D model of their design.

Display ideas

Under a main heading such as 'We visited ____ (name) church to find out what the building tells us about what Christians think is important', the ten important aspects identified on the photocopiable sheet can be written out as labels and displayed. Around each label the photographs and children's statements about areas of the church building could be exhibited. Children's drawings, paintings and written work could also be displayed.

Reference to photocopiable sheet

Photocopiable page 145 identifies ten aspects of Christian life and belief, for which evidence can be found in most churches. Working in pairs, children should write what they saw in the church building for each of these ten aspects, drawing on information and material gained during their visit.

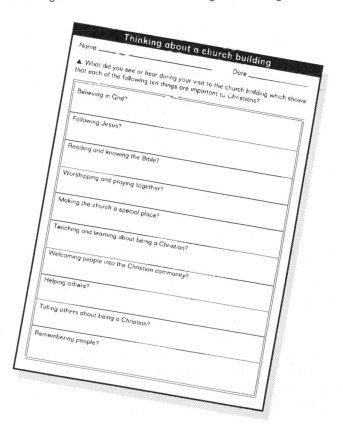

Thinking about a church building

Name _____
What did you see or hear during your visit to the church building which shows that each of the following ten things are important to Christians?
Date _____

Believing in God?

Following Jesus?

Reading and knowing the Bible?

Worshipping and praying together?

Making the church a special place?

Teaching and learning about being a Christian?

Welcoming people into the Christian community?

Helping others?

Telling others about being a Christian?

Remembering people?

WHY IS THE SYNAGOGUE SPECIAL FOR JEWS?

To understand what makes the synagogue a special place for Jews. To know the significance of the ark within the synagogue.

Special place. Community.

†† *Whole class followed by individual work.*
⏰ *Whole class 30 minutes; individual work 30 minutes.*

Key background information

Ideally, this activity should include a video-programme extract showing a synagogue, the ark and the removal of scrolls from the ark. Even for a non-Jew, the opening of an *ark* in a synagogue and the taking out of scrolls can be a majestic and impressive sight.

The design of a particular *synagogue* (the word derives from the Greek word for 'assembly' or 'congregation') will depend upon a number of factors such as age and the type of Jewish community which uses it. In any synagogue, however, the ark will always be the focal point. The Hebrew name for the light which hangs above it is *Ner Tamid* (everlasting light), a reminder that God is always present. The curtains which are drawn when the ark is closed are usually made of a rich material such as velvet, and might be embroidered with two lions (representing the tribe of Judah from which Jews claim descent). The Torah scrolls inside the ark are symbolically 'dressed' with rich covers and silver ornaments.

The synagogue is both a community centre and a place of worship. The fact that many Jews will refer to it by the Yiddish word *shul* (pronounced 'shool' and meaning 'school') is a reminder that the synagogue has always been associated with education and learning. Classes will be held for children in which they learn Hebrew and about the Jewish way of life.

Many excellent poster packs are available on Judaism. The text, drawings and photographs in *The Jewish World* by Douglas Charing are particularly helpful (see 'Useful books and resources', page 109).

Preparation

Decide on an object of your own which is special to you to show the children, if appropriate. Obtain a miniature Torah scroll. Collect pictures, posters, books and video material which are relevant. Make copies of photocopiable page 146, enough for one per child.

Resources needed

Personal object (see 'Preparation'); miniature Torah scroll; pictorial resource material including books; photocopiable page 146; writing and drawing materials.

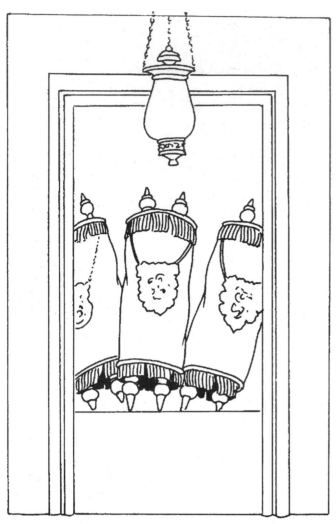

Explain that, as well as being a place where the scrolls can be kept and read from during worship, the synagogue is important to Jews for other reasons. Tell the children that the synagogue is also a place where Jews of all ages meet together. One of the reasons they meet together is to learn about being a Jew, which includes learning how to read the scrolls.

Finally, give each child a copy of photocopiable page 146. Explain that the sheet is in three parts. The first section requires them to choose correct words to complete the sentences. The second section is for them to write about why the synagogue is a special place for Jews and the final section has a space for them to draw a picture of the Torah scrolls.

Suggestion(s) for extension

Ask children to find out more about:
▲ the light that burns above the ark;
▲ the designs embroidered on the curtains in front of the ark;
▲ the objects which cover the scrolls while they are in the ark.

Suggestion(s) for support

Less confident children could read the first part of the photocopiable sheet with an adult, discussing which words might be inserted in the gaps. They could then talk about the importance of the synagogue for Jews with a friend before completing the second part of the sheet.

Assessment opportunities

The accuracy and ease with which children complete the photocopiable sheet will demonstrate the extent of their knowledge and understanding. Further discussion with individual pupils will indicate their grasp of the importance of the synagogue to Jews.

What to do

Gather the children together and show them an object which is special to you and which you keep very carefully in a particular place. Describe where and how it is kept. Give reasons for its special qualities and explain why you keep it in a special place. Ask several children to talk about objects that they have which are special and to describe where they keep them and why they keep them there.

Next, show the children a miniature Torah scroll, reminding them that it is very important to Jews and should be handled with respect. Explain that because Torah scrolls are so special to Jews they keep them in a safe place where they will not be harmed or damaged. Tell them that this place has a special name: it is called an ark and is found in the synagogue, the place where Jews gather to worship. If you have managed to obtain a picture of an ark show this to the children, explaining some of its features:
▲ It is at the front of a synagogue where it can be seen clearly.
▲ It usually has embroidered curtains hanging in front of the doors.
▲ It has a light hanging above it which is always burning.
▲ The inside is richly decorated and often has a light to help you to see the scrolls standing inside.

RELIGIOUS EDUCATION

Opportunities for IT

The children could use an encyclopaedia CD-ROM or a specific religious education CD-ROM, such as the Nelson *Media Aspects of Religion* CD-ROM, to research further information about the synagogue.

Display ideas

Display the children's completed photocopiable sheets and the additional information gathered by those children who carried out the extension activity, together with any pictures or posters, under a title such as 'The ark helps to make the synagogue a special place for Jews'.

Reference to photocopiable sheet

Photocopiable page 146 is divided into three sections and requires the children to complete a passage about the ark in the synagogue, explain the importance of the synagogue for Jews and draw a picture of the scrolls within the ark.

WHY IS A MOSQUE BUILT AS IT IS?

To know the key features associated with a mosque.
To know the purpose of these key features.

Place of worship. Function.

†† *Whole class followed by individual work.*
🕐 *Whole class 40 minutes; individual work 40 minutes.*

Key background information

There is an increasing number of purpose-built mosques in Britain. The most famous example is probably Regent's Park Mosque in London, which has both a golden dome and a minaret. A card model of this mosque is available from Iqra Trust (see 'Useful books and resources', page 109). A number of Muslim artefacts can usefully be included in this activity, such as a qiblah compass and a prayer-mat. A qiblah compass works by the user rotating the compass ring until the needle points to the relevant number for that country – United Kingdom is usually 25 – the silver arrow on the compass case then indicates qiblah. Some prayer-mats are available with a qiblah compass sewn on to them so that the prayer-mat can be positioned facing Makkah. Sometimes the carpet which covers the prayer hall floor is designed in a prayer-mat pattern so that the floor looks as though it is covered by rows and rows of prayer-mats. Recordings of the call to prayer (always using the same words in Arabic) are available. *The Muslim World* by Richard Tames contains an outstanding selection of colour photographs and a very helpful cross-section of a mosque (see 'Useful books and resources', page 109).

In learning about Islam, Arabic terms are frequently encountered. Those used in this activity are: *qiblah* (pronounced 'key-bla'; meaning 'direction', more specifically the direction of the Ka'bah in Makkah), *mihrab* (pronounced 'mi<u>ch</u>-rab', sounding <u>ch</u> as in the Scottish 'loch') and *minbar* (the speaking platform, usually portable and often consisting of three carpeted steps, used during Friday midday prayers).

RELIGIOUS EDUCATION

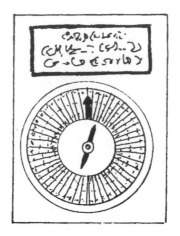

Encountering special places

Preparation

Obtain a qiblah compass and practise using it. Collect together any relevant resources. Make an A3 copy of photocopiable page 147. Make copies of photocopiable page 148, one for each child (enlarging the sheets if necessary).

Resources needed

Qiblah compass; other relevant resources; photocopiable pages 147 and 148; writing and drawing materials; blank paper; scissors; adhesive.

What to do

Gather the children together and show them a qiblah compass. Ask them if they know what it is and what it does. If they are uncertain, or if they confuse it with a standard compass, explain that it is a direction-finder which indicates the direction of a building that is important to Muslims. This building is called the Ka'bah and is in the city of Makkah in Saudi Arabia. Go on to explain that, because the Ka'bah is so important, wherever they live in the world Muslims face it when they pray. Introduce the word 'qiblah' and explain that it is an Arabic word which means 'direction'.

Remind the children that Muslims are supposed to pray five times a day. Demonstrate how the qiblah compass works and find the direction (qiblah) of the Ka'bah in Makkah, telling the children that the compass would be used by Muslims who were travelling and were therefore uncertain of the correct direction for prayer.

Tell the children that another way of finding out the direction is by going to a mosque. Explain that the largest area of a mosque is the prayer hall where Muslims gather to pray. A mosque is built in such a way that, when Muslims face the front wall (the qiblah wall) of this hall, which usually has an alcove called a mihrab in the middle, they know that they are facing the Ka'bah in Makkah.

Show the children the ground plan of a mosque on photocopiable page 147 and the position of the mihrab in the qiblah wall of the prayer hall. Next, point out the other main features of a typical mosque including:

▲ the minbar at the front of the prayer hall – a raised platform from which a talk/sermon is given at the special prayers on a Friday;

▲ a large carpet in the prayer hall – providing a clean place on which to pray;

▲ a dome covering the prayer hall – marking out the prayer hall and mosque as a special place;

▲ a minaret – a tower from which the call to prayer can be issued;

▲ a washing place – so that Muslims can prepare for prayer by washing.

Supplement these facts with other information, as appropriate, using a range of pictorial material such as posters, pictures, artefacts and video programmes (see 'Key background information').

Finally, give each child a copy of photocopiable page 148, explaining that they will be linking together three pieces of information plus a sketch that can form a set of four items – there are six sets all together. When the children have decided how the sets are matched, tell them to cut the different sections out and paste them on to a separate sheet of paper. Each set should contain a sketch, a label, a description of what the sketch shows and an explanation of its function. The children should then use the information to answer the question 'Why is a mosque built as it is?'

RELIGIOUS EDUCATION

Suggestion(s) for extension

When responding to the question 'Why is a mosque built as it is?', children who cope well with this activity can supplement the material on the photocopiable sheet with information gleaned from other sources.

Suggestion(s) for support

Less confident children may need an adult helper or support teacher to work through the various components of a mosque with them again. Enlarging the sheet to A3 will make the cutting and sorting more manipulable.

Assessment opportunities

The results of the written task will provide evidence of the extent of the children's knowledge of the key features of a mosque and the purpose of these key features.

Opportunities for IT

Working as a class, the children can make their own illustrated glossary about the different parts of the mosque (see 'Opportunities for IT', page 83). Extra information could be researched from suitable CD-ROMs.

Framework software such as *My World 2* could be used with the Places of Worship file to allow children to design their own mosque and then use the resulting net to make a 3D model of their design.

Display ideas

Under a title such as 'Why is a mosque built as it is?', a large ground plan of a typical mosque could be displayed, together with the children's descriptions of its features. Any pictures, posters or artefacts (including a qiblah compass with instructions on its use) can also be displayed. An arrow pointing in the direction of Makkah could be placed near the qiblah compass.

Reference to photocopiable sheets

Photocopiable page 147 gives a simplified ground plan of a mosque likely to be found in Britain. This can be increased to A3 size before use with the children. Photocopiable page 148 contains 24 separate items (including sketches) which should be grouped correctly and is for use by the children when writing their final account. It may have to be increased to A3 size for use by some children.

The correct grouping of the different pieces of information is as follows:
▲ Sketch of a dome over a mosque;
A dome;
This is over the prayer hall and might be painted gold outside;
This shows that the prayer hall and the mosque are special.
▲ Sketch of carpet in prayer hall;
The prayer hall;

The largest area in the mosque in which the floor is covered with a carpet;
Muslims gather in here to pray after they have taken off their shoes.
▲ Sketch of section of wall with mihrab;
The qiblah wall;
The wall at the front of the prayer hall;
This shows that the whole room faces in the direction of Makkah.
▲ Sketch of minaret;
The minaret;
A tall tower with a balcony;
The call to prayer is called out from this.
▲ Sketch of minbar;
The minbar;
A raised platform;
A Muslim stands on this to give a talk during special prayers on Friday.
▲ Sketch of some taps;
The washing area;
A room where there is fresh running water;
The place where Muslims can prepare themselves for prayer by washing.

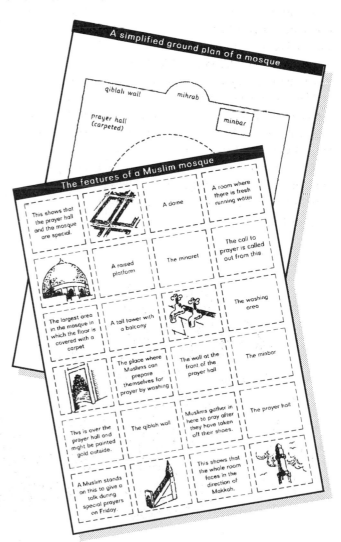

WHY IS THE KA'BAH A SPECIAL PLACE FOR MUSLIMS?

To understand the place of the Ka'bah in Muslim thoughts and feelings. To know the place of the Ka'bah in Muslim pilgrimage.

Focal point. Pilgrimage.

†† *Whole class followed by paired work and then individual work.*

🕐 *Whole class 30 minutes; paired work 10 minutes; individual work 30 minutes.*

Key background information

In that pilgrimage to Makkah (*Hajj* in Arabic) is one of the 'Five Pillars' of Islam, this activity will link well with 'What are the Five Pillars of Islam?', page 61.

Muslims can make a pilgrimage to Makkah (this spelling is usually preferred to 'Mecca') at any time, but Hajj must be during certain days of the twelfth Muslim month. The millions of pilgrims each year follow a set pattern which begins in Makkah with a visit to the Ka'bah but then takes them outside the city to a number of other locations rich with historical and religious associations: they run between the two hills of Marwa and Safa, throw stones at pillars in Mina and stand in prayer on the Plain of Arafat, for example. They will pay a farewell visit to the Ka'bah at the end of the pilgrimage.

Educational books on Islam will usually contain photographs of the Ka'bah, often freeze-framed to show the whirl of Muslims circumnavigating it. The Iqra Trust produces a cardboard model of the Ka'bah and part of the Great Mosque (see 'Useful books and resources', page 109).

The Ka'bah is part of the Islamic world but is also a very emotive place for Muslims (some pilgrims burst into tears when they see it for the first time). The structure of the activity takes this into account, though the choice between follow-up tasks allows the children to be more or less removed from the focus of the activity.

Preparation

Obtain a picture(s) of the Ka'bah and/or a video programme containing scenes of Muslims visiting it during pilgrimage (see 'Useful books and resources', page 109). Collect together books for the children to refer to. Make copies of photocopiable page 149, one for each child.

Resources needed

Picture(s) of the Ka'bah and/or video extract; resource books; photocopiable page 149; writing and drawing materials.

What to do

Show the children a picture or video extract of the Ka'bah in Makkah. Explain that the Ka'bah, a cube-shaped building, marks the place where Muslims believe that Allah (God) was first worshipped. Emphasise that this place is very important to Muslims who:

▲ face towards it during the five daily times of prayer;

▲ often have a representation of it on their prayer-mats;

▲ often have pictures of it in their homes and mosques;

▲ are expected to visit it as part of the pilgrimage which all Muslims are required to go on at least once in their lifetime if they are able;

▲ tell stories connecting the lives of the prophets – including Ibrahim (Abraham) and Muhammad – with it.

Next, move the children into pairs and set them the task of writing down a list of feelings which they think a Muslim pilgrim might experience when seeing the actual Ka'bah –

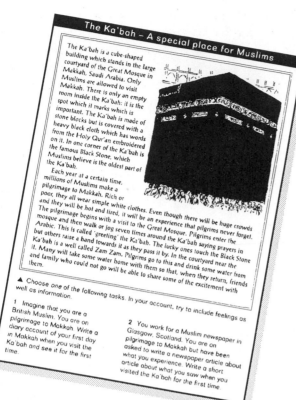

The Ka'bah – A special place for Muslims

The Ka'bah is a cube-shaped building which stands in the large courtyard of the Great Mosque in Makkah, Saudi Arabia. Only Muslims are allowed to visit Makkah. There is only an empty room inside the Ka'bah: it is the spot which it marks which is important. The Ka'bah is made of stone blocks but is covered with a heavy black cloth which has words from the Holy Qur'an embroidered on it. In one corner of the Ka'bah is the famous Black Stone, which Muslims believe is the oldest part of the Ka'bah.

Each year at a certain time, millions of Muslims make a pilgrimage to Makkah. Rich or poor, they all wear simple white clothes. Even though there will be huge crowds and they will be hot and tired, it will be an experience that pilgrims never forget. The pilgrimage begins with a visit to the Great Mosque. Pilgrims enter the mosque and then walk or jog seven times around the Ka'bah saying prayers in Arabic. This is called 'greeting' the Ka'bah. The lucky ones touch the Black Stone but others raise a hand towards it as they pass it by. In the courtyard near the Ka'bah is a well called Zam Zam. Pilgrims go to this and drink some water from it. Many will take some water home with them so that, when they return, friends and family who could not go will be able to share some of the excitement with them.

▲ Choose *one* of the following tasks. In your account, try to include feelings as well as information.

1 Imagine that you are a British Muslim. You are on pilgrimage to Makkah. Write a diary account of your first day in Makkah when you visit the Ka'bah and see it for the first time.

2 You work for a Muslim newspaper in Glasgow, Scotland. You are on pilgrimage to Makkah but have been asked to write a newspaper article about what you experience. Write a short article about what you saw when you visited the Ka'bah for the first time.

rather than just pictures of it – for the first time in his or her life. When the pairs have had sufficient time to complete this task, compile a main list of feelings which have been identified, discussing and analysing them where appropriate.

Finally, give a copy of photocopiable page 149 to each child, explaining that it provides a sketch of the Ka'bah, and some further information about what Muslims do when they visit the Ka'bah on pilgrimage. The children must choose one of the two tasks to complete. Set a time limit for the completion of the task and make additional resource material available.

Suggestion(s) for extension
Children requiring extension work could use the resource material to find out what other special places are visited during the pilgrimage to Makkah.

Suggestion(s) for support
Less confident children might need to discuss their ideas and to be reminded of information which can be used when completing their chosen task.

Assessment opportunities
The written account will indicate the extent to which children have understood the place of the Ka'bah in Muslim thoughts and feelings and know the place of the Ka'bah in Muslim pilgrimage. Quality should be judged in terms of the accuracy of information which has been incorporated as well as how successfully or sensitively the writer has portrayed a range of feelings that a Muslim might experience.

Opportunities for IT
Let the children use an encyclopaedia or specific RE CD-ROM, such as Nelson *Media Aspects of Religion*, to carry out research about the Ka'bah.

Display ideas
Place a picture of the Ka'bah in the centre of a display board and place words around it (compiled from the main list in the activity) which describe feelings that seeing the Ka'bah might evoke in pilgrims. Around this mount a selection of the imaginary diary accounts and newspaper reports. An overall heading such as 'The Ka'bah – a special place for Muslims' might be used.

Reference to photocopiable sheet
Photocopiable page 149 provides a sketch of the Ka'bah and further information about the place of the Ka'bah during Muslim pilgrimage. A choice of two tasks for the children to complete is given at the bottom of the page.

WHAT ARE THE FEATURES OF THE ROOM IN WHICH THE SIKH HOLY BOOK IS PLACED?

To know what physical features of a gurdwara are related to the Sikh holy book. To acquire general information about a Sikh gurdwara.

Design. Special place.

†† *Group work followed by whole class and then individual work.*

🕐 *Group work 20 minutes; whole class 30 minutes; individual work 30 minutes.*

Key background information
There are now a number of purpose-built gurdwaras in Britain. Ideally, this activity should be linked to a visit to one.

A *gurdwara* – literally 'doorway to the Guru' – is specifically the place where the Sikh holy book is housed (see 'Key background information' to the activity 'Where do Sikhs turn for guidance in choosing names', page 57). As such, if a Sikh family were to keep a copy of the Guru Granth Sahib in their own home, the room where it was kept (a specific room would be set aside for it) would be a gurdwara.

The title gurdwara (note that some Sikhs dislike the term 'Sikh temple', preferring the proper title) is more generally used to describe the building used by a Sikh community. Its main room is the worship hall where a copy of the holy book is read from. The features associated with the holy book referred to in the activity – the platform, the stool-like stand (*manji*), the ornate coverings (*romallas*) and cloth canopy (*chanani*) – are part of a living context, of course. Observing Sikhs in a worship hall will reveal other ways in which the holy book is honoured. For example:

▲ The reader sitting behind it (the *Granthi*) will occasionally wave a *chauri*, which looks like a fly-whisk, over the book.

▲ Sikhs entering the worship hall will prostrate themselves in front of the book and often present a gift (such as money, or milk to be used in the kitchen).

The book *The Sikh World* by Daljit Singh and Angela Smith ('Useful books and resources', page 109) contains some excellent colour photographs of gurdwaras and a very useful cross-section of an English gurdwara.

Preparation
Collect resources containing information about the Sikh gurdwara.

Resources needed
Pictures, posters, video extracts and books; writing and drawing materials.

What to do
Divide the children into groups. Give each group a sheet of paper. Ask the groups to imagine that they have a book which is very special to them. It is a very large heavy book. Tell the children that you would like them to design a special room in which this book can be kept. Write the following instructions on the board for the children to refer to.
This book has to be:

▲ read aloud every day;

▲ put away every evening;

▲ looked after while it is open;

▲ treated very carefully.

The book is to be placed in a special room. The importance of the book should be shown through:

▲ where it is placed in the room;

▲ what it is placed on;

▲ having something over the top of it;

▲ having a safe place where it can be put at night.

At the end of an agreed time, call the groups together and ask each one to report back to the whole class, discussing and analysing suggestions as appropriate.

Explain to the children that people called Sikhs have a special book which they keep in a special room. This book is called the Guru Granth Sahib and is special because it contains the teachings of the Gurus (Sikh leaders in the past) and is considered by Sikhs to be their Guru (teacher) today. They therefore treat the book as they did their human Gurus when they were alive. Use pictures, posters, video extracts and books to show what the room in which the Guru Granth Sahib is placed would be like. The main points are:

▲ There would be a raised platform at one end of the room.

▲ The holy book would be placed on a low stand on this platform.

▲ Decorated cloths would be placed over the stand and over the book when not being read.

▲ A cloth canopy would be hanging over the whole platform.

▲ Other decorations (flowers, coloured lights, tinsel) might be placed around the area where the book is placed.

Tell the children that a room like this would usually be inside a building called a gurdwara, which would also have a number of other rooms such as:

▲ a small room where the Guru Granth Sahib is placed at night;

▲ a kitchen and dining area where members of the community eat together when they go to the gurdwara to worship;

▲ space for other activities such as holding classes for children, for keeping a library of books and for holding meetings of the Sikh community.

Finally, ask the children to imagine that they work for a firm of architects which has been asked to design a new gurdwara for the Sikh community. They have been asked to visit a gurdwara and to write a report about the internal use of the building. They should prepare a report, with drawings, paying particular attention to the worship hall – the room where the Guru Granth Sahib is kept during the day.

WHAT MIGHT YOU EXPERIENCE IN A HINDU MANDIR?

To know some of the features and activities associated with a mandir (temple). To understand that visiting a place of worship raises a variety of issues.

Special place. Integrity.

†† *Pairs followed by whole class.*

🕐 *Pairs 30 minutes; whole class 45 minutes.*

Suggestion(s) for extension

The more able children could use the resources to find out further information about rooms other than the worship hall in the gurdwara.

Suggestion(s) for support

Some children may need to be given headings for their architect's report, for example, the worship hall, the eating area, classrooms, the library, the meeting room. They might also need to be reminded of the main features at the front of the worship hall.

Assessment opportunities

The amount of detail and the accuracy which the children incorporate into their imaginary architect's reports will indicate both the extent of the information they have absorbed about a Sikh gurdwara and their understanding of what physical features of a gurdwara are related to the Sikh holy book.

Opportunities for IT

Allow the children to use a drawing package or simple Computer Aided Design (CAD) package to make a plan of their gurdwara. They will need to be shown how to draw lines and shapes and how to add text or colours to their designs. Most packages have a background grid which can be turned to provide a simple scale for the drawing. The 'snap to grid' option will also help children to line up shapes and lines at right angles and is useful for drawing plans of this sort.

Children could use CD-ROMs to search for pictures and other ideas for their designs.

Key background information

The emphasis of this activity is placed not only on learning about a Hindu *mandir* but also on exploring the type of responses that a non-Hindu visiting one for the first time might experience. The young girl in the imaginary account is thus a device to enable the children to think about their own responses and feelings.

Many of the things which are touched upon lightly in this account could be gone into in much greater detail. In brief:

▲ Shoe removal and hand-washing are marks of respect.

▲ The pictures on the walls would be of Hindu deities and gurus.

▲ The writing would be texts from sacred scriptures such as the *Bhagavad Gita*, the language probably Sanskrit.

▲ The shrine at the front of the worship hall would have images (*murtis*) of Hindu deities, almost certainly including blue-skinned Krishna.

▲ The elephant-headed deity is Ganesha, thought to provide help in overcoming obstacles.

▲ Hanuman is the monkey warrior who faithfully served Rama and Sita, as in the Divali story.

▲ The act of worship involving the waving of candles (more accurately, a many-wicked lamp using *ghee* – clarified butter), singing and the ringing of a bell is called *arti*.

▲ Devotees bring offerings to the deities, the coconut being a symbol of good luck.

▲ The man in white would be the priest, the expert in sacred rituals and texts connected with worship.

▲ Hindus spread their hands over the flames and then wipe their faces and hair with their hands to absorb some of the goodness of the light into themselves.

▲ Some food which has been blessed is given back to worshippers as a gift (*prashad*).

A number of religious and cultural artefacts could be used to support this activity such as incense sticks and images of Ganesha and Hanuman.

Preparation

Make copies of photocopiable pages 150 and 151, one for each child. Collect resources relating to Hindu temples.

RELIGIOUS EDUCATION

Encountering special places

Resources needed

Photocopiable pages 150 and 151; books, posters, pictures and video-programme extracts; writing materials.

What to do

Ask the children to work with a partner, making sure that one partner in each pair is a competent reader. Give each child a copy of photocopiable page 150, telling them that it contains an account of a non-Hindu girl visiting a Hindu temple (mandir) for the first time. Ask them to read her account carefully. When the children have done this, give out copies of photocopiable page 151. Still working with their partner, ask them to answer the questions. Give them a specified time in which to complete this task.

At the end of the time allowed, bring the children together and work through the sheet, question by question, allowing time for discussion as necessary.

Next, ask the children if they have any questions about the account (see 'Key background information'). Then, either show the children a short extract from a video programme which features the Hindu temple (or worshipping taking place in it) or let the children look at books and posters.

Finally, set aside a time for any last questions and comments the children may have regarding what they have seen or discovered.

Suggestion(s) for extension

Children requiring extension work could be asked to find out more about what happens during arti (see 'Key background information'), building on the brief general description given in the account of the visit.

Suggestion(s) for support

Some children may need help in thinking through their responses to the questions on photocopiable page 151. If necessary, they could be given further time to formulate and write their answers following the whole-class discussion.

Assessment opportunities

The quality of the discussion and the range of questions which the children ask will provide evidence of the extent to which they have acquired knowledge of the features and activities associated with a mandir. The written responses

to the questions on photocopiable page 151 – ranging from short simple responses with few reasons to longer more subtle answers supported by a number of explanations – will provide evidence as to whether the children have understood that visiting a place of worship raises a variety of issues.

Opportunities for IT

This activity could be extended, with the class working together to make a multimedia presentation about the mandir. Groups of children can select aspects of the mandir and research further information on their topic. They could then design two or three linked computer pages about their topic. Much of the page design work could take place away from the computer using photocopied templates of the screen.

The pages could contain text; pictures, which can be drawn using an art or drawing package, taken from clip-art collections or CD-ROMs, or scanned from their own line drawings or photographs; and sounds recorded using a microphone attached to the computer.

Prior to the lesson you may like to set up a structure and title page for the presentation so that clicking on Krishna, for example, would take the user to the pages about Krishna. As this requires the integration of several forms of information, children will need support when tackling this type of work for the first time.

Reference to photocopiable sheets

Photocopiable page 150 gives an imaginary account of a first visit to a Hindu mandir by a non-Hindu. The children read this account and then answer the questions which follow on photocopiable page 151.

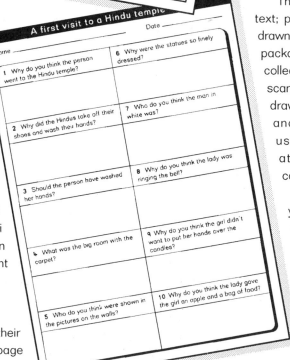

Expressing what is important

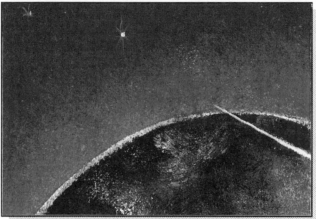

In a whole range of intentional and unintentional ways, people express what is of importance and value to them. At the individual level, the painter, sculptor, musician and poet are all striving to express through their chosen medium a range of emotions and interpretations. At the group level, rituals embody a range of meanings (conventions and beliefs, values and ideals) even though these might only be apparent to the knowing observer.

Through religious practice, individuals and groups seek to give expression to their highest and deepest beliefs and aspirations – in prayer and worship, in the stories they tell, in the ways in which they take leave of the dead and dying, in the art forms which all religions have given rise to. In that much is an attempt to express the inexpressible, symbolism abounds.

The activities in this chapter cover a range of modes of expression and a variety of religious beliefs and practice. At times, there is a body of knowledge for the children to learn: the types of crosses to be found within Christianity, the reasons why calligraphy and Arabesque have arisen within Islam, for example. But there is also a strong emphasis on *applying* what has been learned so that the children not only learn about how others seek to express themselves but also engage in the act or art of expression themselves. So, for instance, tasks include designing a 'new' kind of cross to meet a specific need, and creating a design for the front wall of a school hall which would 'speak' to members of the school community as they gather together.

RELIGIOUS
EDUCATION

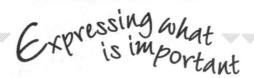

WHAT BELIEFS ARE REPRESENTED IN A CHRISTIAN GRAVEYARD?

To understand some Christian beliefs and ideas about life and death. To know and understand some examples of Christian symbolism.

Symbolism. Life after death.

†† *Whole class before the visit, individual work during the visit, whole class after the visit.*

🕐 *Whole class 20 minutes; individual as appropriate; whole class 30 minutes.*

Key background information

This activity would link well with those involving a church visit (see 'How can a Church reveal what Christians think is important?', page 81) and finding out about Holy Week (see 'How do Christians remember the events of Holy Week?', page 66). It might also suggest opportunities for visiting cemeteries used for non-Christian burials.

Ambivalent attitudes towards death and dying within contemporary Western society might make this activity seem, at first glance, a surprising one. Yet, graveyards and cemeteries (burial grounds which have not grown up around a particular church building) provide a fascinating glimpse into a range of social trends and beliefs: changes in family size, the frequency of infant mortality in past generations, changes in fashions for names, death in wartime, religious ideas and imagery. A particular graveyard will be heavily influenced by the religious beliefs of the group that uses it.

Roman Catholic gravestones will make frequent reference to praying for the dead, for example, while older Quaker burial grounds will not use the names of months but only their number – the '9th month' being September, and so on. Graveyards also reflect the prevailing culture. Note, for example, the continental practice of placing photographs of the deceased on the gravestone. Today, financial considerations and ease of graveyard maintenance have led to greater simplicity and uniformity.

This activity focuses upon the gravestones and associated flora found in graveyards. Inscriptions on gravestones will make frequent use of biblical quotations and a range of imagery to express 'death, but not death', such as going to sleep, taken away, being called, waiting, and so on. Epitaphs can be full of emotion; some are humorous (books of 'grave humour' have been published). Flora in graveyards is said to reflect beliefs in life after death, for example the evergreen yew tree is traditionally associated with English graveyards, while carved or real daffodils (which produce life from their apparently dead bulbs) are frequently to be seen.

Preparation

Make a preliminary visit to a graveyard and, if possible, seek permission for your class to visit from the incumbent of the church. Make copies of photocopiable page 152, enough for one per child (or make and photocopy a worksheet of your own).

Resources needed

Photocopiable page 152 (or worksheet); clipboards; loaded camera; writing materials.

What to do

Before the visit, discuss with the children what they are going to look for when they get to the graveyard.

▲ Remind the children that they must be respectful when looking at the graves and that there may be people visiting gravesides who would be upset by inappropriate behaviour.

▲ They will need to look for evidence of what Christians believe and think about life and death. Explain that Christians believe that death is not the end and that something goes on beyond death. They believe this because of what happened to Jesus at Easter.

▲ Evidence might be found in the form of: writing on gravestones, pictures on gravestones, carvings, types of plants found in graveyards.

Give each child a copy of photocopiable page 152, extra paper if necessary, and explain the tasks on the sheet.

Take the children on the visit and photograph both the children carrying out their tasks and examples of different gravestones and graveyard flora. Upon your return to school, discuss the examples you have gathered with the children and talk about their meaning and implications for Christian belief.

RELIGIOUS EDUCATION

and flora together with explanatory comments. Some of the inscriptions and pictures could be reproduced on small card 'gravestones' which could be placed on a horizontal piece of card to form a miniature graveyard.

Suggestion(s) for extension

Children could be asked to look for evidence of changes in ideas and practice over the years, for example larger gravestones were much more common a century ago.

Suggestion(s) for support

On the preliminary visit which you make to the graveyard, examples which can be used to complete the photocopiable sheet will already have been identified. Children can be pointed towards these, and their meaning discussed during the visit.

Assessment opportunities

The examples which the children enter on to their photocopiable sheets, the written explanations which they give and the quality of the classroom discussion after the visit will provide general evidence of the extent to which they have become aware of Christian symbolism and of Christian beliefs about life and death.

Display ideas

Use a general heading such as 'We visited a graveyard to find out what Christians believe about life and death'. One part of the display can be labelled 'How we worked' and could show photographs of children during the visit, together with several mounted examples of completed photocopiable sheets. The other part of the display, labelled 'What we found out', can give examples of inscriptions, pictures, carvings

Reference to photocopiable sheet

Photocopiable page 152 is for use during a visit to a graveyard and requires the children to find four different types of evidence of Christian beliefs and ideas about life and death.

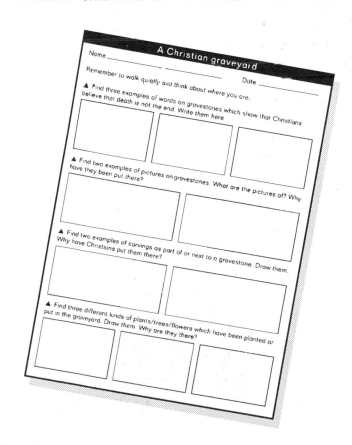

HOW DO PEOPLE EXPRESS THEMSELVES THROUGH PATTERNS?

To understand why Muslims use Arabesque and calligraphy. To express beliefs, values and ideas in pictorial form.

Pattern. Expression.

†† *Whole class followed by individual or paired work.*

🕐 *Whole class 20 minutes; individual/paired work 40 minutes.*

Key background information
Though representation of people and living creatures is not unknown in the art of Muslims (in Persian paintings, for example), Islamic art has generally been 'non-representational'. The representation of people and living creatures has been avoided, and even the use of floral designs, on prayer-mats and tiles for example, has been stylised rather than realistic. This instinctive move against representational art is rooted in the Muslim belief that *shirk*, imitating Allah or putting something in Allah's place, should be avoided at all costs. It is for the same reason that the Prophet Muhammad is not represented. In the film about the Prophet's life, *The Message*, the Prophet's voice is heard but he is never seen.

The Muslim artistic urge has expressed itself primarily through calligraphy and Arabesque. Calligraphy uses the Arabic words of the Qur'an, and many different styles have developed (such as the *Kufic*), some square and angular, others more curved and full of flourishes. Arabesque is recognisable by its use of symmetrical patterns and motifs which, when covering a large area, such as the inside or outside of a mosque dome, can be breathtaking. It is sometimes said that the sense of profound order created by Arabesque can remind a Muslim of the profound universal order which Allah has created. A building such as the 'Dome of the Rock' in Jerusalem shows both Arabesque and calligraphy at their finest.

Many books are available which give colour photographs of Islamic art, such as *The Muslim World* by Richard Tames. The Iqra Trust produces a card model of the Dome of the Rock (see 'Useful books and resources', page 109 for both these references).

This activity not only provides an opportunity for children to learn about Islamic art but also to apply what they have learned in a design task.

Preparation
Make copies of photocopiable page 153, one for each child. Gather together books and other resources containing examples of Islamic patterns.

Resources needed
Photocopiable page 153; writing and drawing materials. For the extension activity – books, posters, pictures depicting Muslim art.

What to do
Give each child a copy of photocopiable page 153. Ask them to look at the patterns on the sheet closely and then to say:

▲ what they think the patterns are;

▲ whether they can see different kinds of pattern;

▲ whether they have seen patterns like this before;

▲ whether there is anything else they notice about the patterns.

Next, explain what the patterns are by covering the following points:

▲ These are the kinds of pattern which Muslims have used for well over 1000 years.

▲ Patterns like these would be found outside and inside Muslim buildings like mosques.

▲ Some of the patterns use Arabic writing taken from the Qur'an and decorate it beautifully.

▲ When writing is made aesthetically pleasing like this it is called 'calligraphy'.

▲ Muslims have wanted to make the words of the Qur'an beautiful because they believe that these words were given by Allah (God) and are therefore very special.

▲ The other patterns on the sheet use repeated shapes and symmetry.

▲ When Muslims do this it is called 'Arabesque'.

▲ Muslims do not usually draw or paint pictures of people and other living creatures because they believe that this would be like copying Allah who made living things.

▲ Instead, Muslim artists have used Arabesque to show that the world is a beautiful place which Allah has made.

Finally, explain that sometimes Muslim artists have deliberately incorporated a mistake into their work as a reminder that only Allah is perfect.

Having highlighted that the way in which buildings are decorated will sometimes reflect what people believe and think is important, set the following task for the children. It can be completed either individually or in pairs.

A school has decided that its hall should be decorated, paying particular attention to the front wall that faces the children and teachers during assemblies. The school would like the decoration of this wall to include patterns and calligraphy which remind people of what is important about school. Tell the children that the words and patterns must be connected with school so that, for example, words connected with learning could be used in the calligraphy, a pattern could use books and pencils for shapes. While the children are carrying out this task, discuss with them why they have chosen particular words or patterns.

Suggestion(s) for extension

Children could go on to look for examples of Muslim calligraphy and Arabesque in books and other sources and to record any further information about them which they find, such as the titles of different styles of Muslim calligraphy.

Suggestion(s) for support

At the transition point between the whole class and individual/ paired work, it may be necessary to look at the photocopiable sheet again with some children in order to ensure that they know the difference between calligraphy and Arabesque and that they understand why Muslims use them.

Assessment opportunities

Discussions with the children while they are working on the task will reveal how far they have understood the Muslim use of calligraphy and Arabesque and have been able to transfer this understanding to their own design task. Observe whether the shape of the calligraphy and the type of symmetrical pattern created is linked to underlying ideas.

Opportunities for IT

Encourage the children to use a drawing or art package to create their own patterns based on Muslim designs. Demonstrate the ways in which a simple shape can be repeated, by copying it repeatedly and then moving the duplicated shape to fit with other shapes, possibly rotating or flipping it to create the pattern. The children could add colour to their designs as well. Displaying the background grid and making shapes 'snap to grid' will enable the children to make the pattern more regular.

Children could use Framework software such as *My World 2* with the Eid file to explore and make other Muslim patterns.

RELIGIOUS
EDUCATION

Display ideas

Under a heading such as 'Expression through patterns', devote one part of a display to Islamic patterns. Give the children enlarged examples of the calligraphy and Arabesque from photocopiable page 153, and ask them to colour them in after they have referred to the examples found by the extension group. Use the other part of the display to show the children's own ideas for the school hall wall with written explanations about why particular words, patterns and shapes were chosen.

Reference to photocopiable sheet

Photocopiable page 153 gives examples of Muslim Arabesque and calligraphy to stimulate discussion during the first part of the activity and to suggest ideas for the second.

Muslim calligraphy and Arabesque

⬛ HOW ARE IMPORTANT EVENTS REMEMBERED?

To understand that Remembrance Day fulfils a variety of roles and needs. To understand that ritual and ceremony are a means by which people express feelings.

Remembrance. Ritual.

†† *Whole class followed by group work.*

🕐 *Whole class 20 minutes; group work 30 minutes.*

Key background information

It was at the eleventh hour of the eleventh month, 1918, that the Armistice was signed in Marshall Foch's railway coach, near Compiègne, bringing the Great War to an end. It has been estimated that the war cost around nine million lives, with a further 27 million injured. The Cenotaph War Memorial in Whitehall, London, was unveiled by King George V on 11 November, 1920. The 35-foot memorial (the word cenotaph means 'empty tomb') was designed by Sir Edwin Lutyens. It was on 11 November 1921 that the British Legion held the first Poppy Day.

The first part of this activity could be supplemented by material such as a video recording of the London Cenotaph service.

The second part of the activity moves beyond looking at what happens during the British Remembrance Day to a practical exploration of the emotional and other needs that an occasion such as Remembrance Day meets. This is placed in a school setting so that the children can identify with the task.

RELIGIOUS EDUCATION

Preparation
Obtain a red poppy.

Resources needed
Red poppy; writing materials.

What to do
Show the children a red poppy and ask them what they know about Remembrance Day and the time of year when poppies are worn. Build on the children's existing knowledge, making sure that the following points are covered:

▲ Poppies grew on some of the battlefields of the First World War.

▲ The red poppy is used as a reminder of all the people who died or were injured fighting in wars.

▲ The money from the sale of poppies is used to support those affected by war.

▲ There are many ceremonies and customs on Remembrance Day itself, both national, for example laying of the wreaths at the Cenotaph, two minute's silence, and local, such as laying of wreaths on war memorials, parades, and so on.

Ask the children why they think these things are done each year, and what feelings they might arouse in the people who carry them out.

Next, divide the children into groups and ask each group to imagine that something serious has happened in school that needs to be remembered each year, for instance part of the school burned down and had to be rebuilt. Each group should decide what it is that has happened; why it needs to be remembered; and how it will be remembered.

Set the groups a time limit for the completion of this task, at the end of which they should explain to the rest of the class what they have decided.

Suggestion(s) for extension
Children could write an account of someone going to the Cenotaph on Remembrance Day describing what he saw and how he felt.

Suggestion(s) for support
Children who find the activity difficult could work together as a group with a support teacher or adult helper prompting and providing ideas as necessary.

Assessment opportunities
The children's understanding of ritual and ceremony as means of expressing feelings will be indicated by the way in which the groups are able to identify a situation which 'calls' for remembrance and can create a number of appropriate rituals which would appear to meet the emotional and other needs of participants.

Opportunities for IT
Ask the children to use a word processor to design a commemorative plaque for their chosen event. They should look at other plaques before deciding on what needs to be said and how the plaque will look. Encourage the children to use different font styles and sizes for the plaque. They should also be shown how to position text using the centre and justify commands instead of the spacebar to move text around the screen. The completed plaque can be printed out and used as part of a class display.

Assembly ideas
The information from the first part of this activity can be incorporated into an assembly focusing on Remembrance Day.

RELIGIOUS EDUCATION

WHY ARE THERE DIFFERENT KINDS OF CROSS?

To know the titles and meanings of a number of crosses. To design and explain the meaning of a variation of the Christian cross.

Symbolism. Meaning.

†† *Whole class followed by individual work.*

🕐 *Whole class 30 minutes; individual work 30 minutes.*

Key background information

Familiarity with the cross can sometimes mean it is possible to forget that Christianity has, from the beginning, used a Roman device for execution as its major sign or symbol. Historically, however, it is likely that Jesus himself had to carry the cross-beam prior to his crucifixion, the vertical member being left in place at the site of execution. Thus a T-shape cross (a form which is sometimes used and called 'St Anthony's Cross') might be more historically accurate than the form most often seen (the 'Latin Cross').

Many more forms of cross than those listed on the photocopiable sheet can be found and are sometimes quite local in use. The 'Lichfield Cross', for example, is associated with Lichfield Cathedral in Staffordshire.

The cross can serve both as a 'sign' or a 'symbol'. As a sign, it is simply an indication that something or someone is Christian, as with a cross on a building, a book or a lapel badge. Symbols, however, move beyond information giving to encouraging a search for meaning. A symbol can mean many things, and new meanings are always waiting to be discovered.

The second part of the activity provides an opportunity for children to understand the symbolic dimension of crosses through designing one to meet a specific need and then to justify its design.

Preparation

Obtain examples of the Latin and Celtic crosses. Either obtain examples or produce illustrations of the other four types of cross shown on photocopiable page 154. Make copies of photocopiable page 154, one for each child.

Resources needed

Examples and/or illustrations of crosses; photocopiable page 154; writing and drawing materials.

What to do

Show the class a wooden Latin cross. Encourage responses by asking questions:
▲ What is it?
▲ Where would you expect to see one?

RELIGIOUS EDUCATION

▲ What does it make you think of?

▲ Who would find it important?

Explain that this shape of cross, probably the most common one in the Western world, is called the 'Latin Cross'.

Next, show the children another type of cross. What differences can they see between this cross and the Latin cross? Incorporate the children's observations and prior knowledge when explaining what this cross is called and what its origin is. Repeat this process until all six types of cross shown on photocopiable page 154 have been covered.

Explain to the children that crosses can identify something as Christian but they can also remind people of important ideas and beliefs and make them think more deeply about these issues. Return to the Celtic Cross to illustrate this.

▲ The Latin Cross shape 'within' the Celtic Cross could remind a Christian that, in Jesus, God (represented by the vertical line) and human kind (represented by the horizontal line) come together.

▲ The circle at the centre (the 'ring of glory') is a reminder that the cross is something holy and 'special'.

▲ The interlacing 'Celtic' patterns on the cross which seem never to end could make a person think about God, who has no beginning and no end.

Finally, give each child a copy of photocopiable page 154, explaining that they should connect each cross with the correct description before completing the design task on an A4 sheet of paper.

Suggestion(s) for extension

Ask the children to produce an illustrated list of the different places where crosses may be found. These might include lapel badges, prayer books and Bibles, food, buildings, memorials, gravestones, necklaces and other types of jewellery. Photographs found in reference books on Christianity might be a useful starting point for this.

Suggestion(s) for support

When designing their own crosses, some children may need to discuss with an adult the ideas they wish to incorporate and how these might be represented in the design.

Assessment opportunities

The first part of completed photocopiable page 154 will show to what extent the children know the titles and meanings of a number of crosses. The detail and the depth of explanation given in response to the design task will show to what extent they have understood the symbolic nature of a Christian cross.

Opportunities for IT

Let the children use a drawing package or art package to design their own crosses. They could add colours or patterns to the cross according to the purpose for their particular cross.

Display ideas

Under a heading such as 'Christian crosses', the different types of cross can be displayed alongside accompanying cards which explain their names and meanings. The work of those children who carried out the extension activity can be displayed around the crosses. Nearby, and under a second heading such as 'We designed crosses to represent different ideas', examples of the crosses produced by the children can be displayed.

Reference to photocopiable sheet

Photocopiable page 154 consists of two parts. The first section requires the children to match each description to a cross. The second section, which allows a choice, sets a design task in which the children are required to design a cross for an imaginary Christian group, who would like their designs to suggest key ideas – that Christianity is worldwide, encourages care for the environment and is for people of all ages.

WHY DO PEOPLE PRAY DIFFERENTLY?

To understand the link between bodily positions and inward attitudes and beliefs. To encourage respect for those who have different beliefs and customs.

Prayer. Gesture.

Whole class followed by individual work.

Whole class 30 minutes; individual work 30 minutes.

Key background information

The SCAA Model Syllabuses documents (see Introduction, page 8) list 'respect' among the attitudes which religious education should be seeking to promote. The attitude of respect includes 'respecting those who have different beliefs and customs to one's own' and 'avoidance of ridicule'. Looking at the unfamiliar, such as physical positions adopted in devotional activity, can evoke amusement in some children. Realistically, it might be that this is a stage which children have to pass through in order to come to terms with diversity and uncertainty. Each teacher will have to decide on how best to move the children to a position where they can begin to ask serious questions about such subject matter.

Within Christianity, there is a wide range of belief and practice associated with prayer. Within Islam, by contrast, there are a number of basic positions which Muslims learn. On photocopiable page 155 illustration No. 5, for example, is a position which many Muslims adopt during *du'a* – personal prayer at any time and in one's own words and language. Illustration No. 6 is one of the basic positions used during *salah* – set prayer which occurs five times daily. Technically, this position is referred to as *sujud* and demonstrates the 'servant' status of a Muslim in relation to the greatness of Allah.

Preparation

Make copies of photocopiable page 155, one for each child. Gather support material such as pictures, posters, extracts from video programmes.

Resources needed

Photocopiable page 155; adhesive; scrap paper; writing materials; support material (see 'Preparation').

What to do

Ask the children to think about different ways in which people can show that they are praying; hands together, eyes closed, kneeling, hands raised in the air. Explain that physical positions that people use can:

▲ show how they feel when they are talking to God;

▲ be a way of concentrating and putting them in the mood for praying;

▲ be habitual (they use them 'automatically').

Give each child a copy of photocopiable page 155 and look at each of the illustrated prayer positions in turn, beginning with those that the children have already suggested. Distribute scrap paper to let the children make notes (explain that these will be referred to later), and discuss each prayer position, making sure that the following points are covered:

▲ No. 1, hands together: this is used by many Christians, who might teach their children to do this.

RELIGIOUS EDUCATION

Expressing what is important

▲ No. 2, kneeling on a cushion: many Christians kneel to pray, lowering themselves in this way to show that they are in the presence of God.

▲ No. 3, hands raised to the sky: some Christians do this when they are praying and worshipping with others to express their joy and deep feelings.

▲ No. 4, standing with head covered: Orthodox male Jews sometimes cover their head with their *tallit* (prayer-shawl) to indicate that they want to be alone with God.

▲ No. 5, kneeling with hands raised at shoulder level: Muslims might do this to show that they want to receive Allah's blessings.

▲ No. 6, kneeling with forehead touching the ground: when Muslims do this during their five daily prayers, they are placing themselves low down near to the ground to show the greatness of Allah.

Ask the children to complete the activity by cutting out the pictures, pasting them on to a blank sheet of paper and then, next to each picture, writing a paragraph which includes:
▲ the religious group that uses this position;
▲ a description of the position itself;
▲ an explanation of what the position might show about the person's beliefs.

Suggestion(s) for extension
Ask children to find out about the other physical positions adopted by a Muslim during set prayer each day and what they might express about a Muslim's beliefs.

Suggestion(s) for support
Before starting to write their descriptions, children who experience difficulties could be brought together as a group with a support teacher or adult helper. They could read through their notes together to make sure that they have enough understanding of the material to complete the final part of the activity.

Assessment opportunities
The completed final task will indicate whether the children have understood the link between bodily positions and inward attitudes and beliefs. At best, the descriptions will make a number of links between the physical position being adopted by the person in each picture and their beliefs and attitudes (including suggestions which were not discussed in the first part of the lesson). The degree to which the children are

Positions that people adopt for prayer

aware that they should be respectful towards those people with different beliefs and customs can only be gauged by the seriousness with which the whole class is able to participate in the activity.

Display ideas
Under a heading such as 'Why do people pray differently?', each of the pictures shown on the photocopiable sheet can be enlarged, coloured and mounted. A description and explanation could be placed alongside each picture. Other pictorial material such as pictures and posters could also be displayed.

Reference to photocopiable sheet
Photocopiable page 155 provides drawings of six people adopting prayer positions taken from the Christian, Jewish and Muslim traditions. The children make notes on each one, before writing about its religious significance.

WHAT DO HINDUS LEARN FROM THE STORY OF KRISHNA'S BIRTH?

To understand that stories convey teachings. To detect teachings within a story.

Symbolism. Teaching.

†† *Whole class followed by paired work, returning to whole class.*
🕐 *Whole class 10 minutes; paired work 30 minutes; whole class 20 minutes.*

Key background information
This would link well with the activity based on the story of Krishna, the butter-thief.

A number of Krishna stories, with illustrations by Michael Foreman, are to be found in Madhur Jaffrey's *Seasons of Splendour* in which she also talks about the role of story in her own childhood (see 'Useful books and resources', page 109).

Within Eastern traditions, the feet are of particular importance. The feet of a guru (spiritual teacher) might be touched by a disciple. It is said of the new-born Siddhartha Gautama (the future Buddha) that wherever he placed his feet, a lotus blossom bloomed. So, too, in this story, when

Krishna's feet touched the troubled waters of the river, the waters immediately became quiet.

Story has always had a profound role in passing on values and beliefs to the next generation. For Hindu children in Britain, this story, particularly dramatised versions which are available in video format, remains a significant way in which their Hindu identity is formed, (see *Hindu Children in Britain* by Robert Jackson and Eleanor Nesbitt 'Useful books and resources', page 109).

Preparation
Obtain a picture or image of Krishna. Make copies of photocopiable page 156, one for each pair.

Resources needed
Picture or image of Krishna; photocopiable page 156; writing materials.

What to do
Show the children a picture or image of Krishna. Explain that Krishna is a Hindu deity and is very important to many Hindus. Tell them that many stories are told about Krishna's life and that in listening to and retelling these stories, Hindus remember why Krishna is special.

Divide the children into pairs and give each pair a copy of photocopiable page 156. Tell them to read the story, discuss it and then underline the parts which they think teach Hindus that Krishna is special. On the reverse of the sheet, they should then write their reasons for identifying those sections that they have underlined.

The birth of Krishna

There was once a wicked king called Kans who ruled over a kingdom in India. Devaki, his younger sister, was getting married to Vasudev. Just as the wedding celebrations were coming to an end, Kans heard a voice saying that a baby born to Devaki and Vasudev would eventually kill him. Kans was angry, and threw his sister and her new husband into prison. After a while, Kans heard from the prison guards that Devaki had had a baby daughter. Kans ordered the baby to be killed. As the prison guards tried to kill the baby girl, she turned and said, 'I am not the baby you are looking for. Another yet to be born will kill the king.'

Six other children were born, and the king ordered each one to be killed, but each one said the same thing.

The eighth baby to be born was a boy whom Devaki called Krishna. No sooner had he been born than Vasudev heard a voice telling him to take his baby son across the river to his sister Yashoda's house and exchange him for her new-born baby girl. Vasudev wrapped up baby Krishna and placed him in a basket. To his amazement, he found the cell doors were unlocked and that all the prison guards were in a deep sleep. Vasudev carried baby Krishna to the banks of the river which was deep and fast-flowing. Vasudev lifted the baby in the basket above his head to keep him dry and safe. He waded into the river and the waters rose higher and higher. Soon they were lapping around Vasudev's chin, who thought that they would both drown. Baby Krishna gently lowered his foot over the side of the basket until it touched the foaming waters. At once, the river became still and parted to allow father and son to walk safely across to the other side. As soon as they had crossed, the waters closed behind them.

Vasudev went straight to Yashoda's house and told her what had happened. They swapped Krishna for Yashoda's new-born baby girl and, leaving Krishna with Yashoda, Vasudev returned with the baby girl to the prison cell.

Next morning, when the king heard that Devaki had had another baby, he again sent for the baby to be killed. But before the guards could kill the baby, she shouted, 'Krishna is born already and is safe far away!' When Kans heard that he had been tricked, he was very angry and he gave an order that all baby boys in his kingdom under the age of 12 months were to be killed. He did not know that Krishna was safe because he was across the river in another kingdom.

Finally, bring the children together as a whole class, compare underlined sections and come to an agreement about the section which teaches Hindus the most important thing about Krishna.

Suggestion(s) for extension
The most able children could either be given or asked to find another Krishna story (see 'Key background information') and be asked to identify parts of that story which show that Krishna is special for Hindus.

Suggestion(s) for support
When arranging the paired work, ensure that the less confident readers are working with the more confident ones.

Assessment opportunities
General evidence that the children have understood that stories convey readings and that they are able to detect teachings within a story will be provided by listening to the discussions between the pairs and by the whole-class discussion at the end of the activity.

Reference to photocopiable sheet
Photocopiable page 156 provides a retelling of the story of the birth of Krishna for use by pairs of children, whose task is to underline the parts of the story which they think teach Hindus that Krishna is special before writing the reasons for their conclusions on the reverse of the sheet.

HOW CAN A COMMUNITY EXPRESS MEANING?

To understand how symbolism can be an expression of feelings and experiences. To encourage the ability to see the world through the eyes of others.

Symbolism. Community.

†† *Whole class followed by group work.*

🕐 *Whole class 30 minutes; group work as appropriate.*

Key background information

It would generally be agreed that good religious education moves beyond 'mere' learning about what happens in different religious traditions to engage children with issues and experiences which can give rise to a variety of responses, including religious ones. As such, learning about the symbolism that is used in different religious traditions is not sufficient in itself: a context needs to be found for children to understand symbolism 'from the inside' and to *create* symbol. The story of 'The lake that turned to ice' provides such a context.

There are many ways in which this story can be used and developed. In this activity there is great potential for moving beyond planning and designing to creating and dramatising. Many children instinctively draw on their existing fund of knowledge – relating to festivals, sacred buildings, symbolism, ritual, and so on – to use symbolism in a very creative way. This was demonstrated by the child who designed and then made a model of a special building in the shape of a fish; the building faced towards the rising sun, and at its centre had a special gold-coloured table in the shape of an apple, which was topped by a 'spire' shaped like a block of ice.

Preparation

Make a copy of photocopiable page 157 and become familiar with the story.

Resources needed

Photocopiable page 157; writing and drawing materials.

What to do

Tell the children that they are going to hear a story about an imaginary village, the people who lived there and what happened to them. Tell or read the story on photocopiable page 157.

Discuss the story, incorporating the children's own observations and ideas. Then, in order to prepare for the next part of the activity, ask the children to respond to a number of questions such as:
▲ Why do you think the villagers had to give something back to the lake?
▲ Why do you think the villagers chose apple juice?
▲ Do you think that any of the villagers would have been tempted to eat the rainbow fish?
▲ Why didn't they?
▲ Why do you think the villagers felt a need to remember?
▲ Why do you think the villagers didn't feel bitter?

Next, divide the children into groups and give each group one of four tasks, offering suggestions for the kinds of things each group might consider:
▲ to plan what might happen at the annual festival (there may be special food, lighting, drama, storytelling, processions, music);
▲ to design the special building incorporating aspects of shape, decoration, colour, direction facing, number of rooms, purpose of rooms;
▲ to plan what might happen at the weekly meeting. Would there be words, silence, music, actions, adults and children, men and women?
▲ to design the clothing which would be worn by the people who looked after the building and any special objects they would carry, for example colour, signs, symbols, headwear, fabric, patterns.

Allow the groups sufficient time to carry out one of the tasks and when they have finished ask them to explain to the rest of the class what they have done and why.

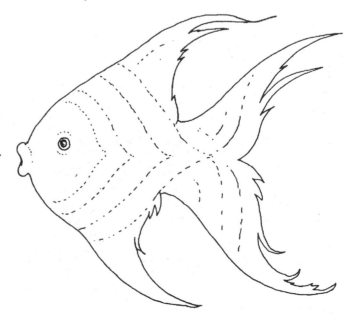

RELIGIOUS EDUCATION

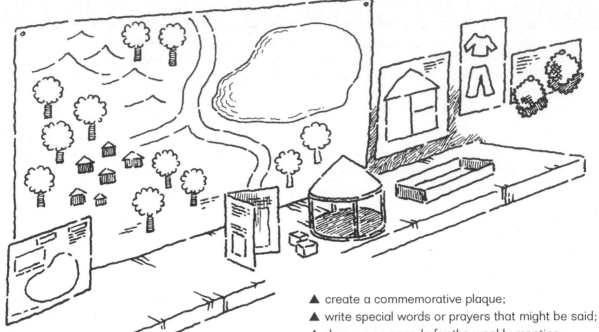

▲ create a commemorative plaque;

▲ write special words or prayers that might be said;

▲ draw up an agenda for the weekly meeting.
    They could use an art or drawing package to:

▲ design the plan of a special building, or to draw an external view of what they think the building will look like;

▲ design clothing to be worn by the people who look after the building;

▲ draw pictures of the objects they would carry;

▲ create an imaginary map of the village;

▲ design a logo or symbolic picture to represent the event, which could be used as a logo or crest for the village.

Suggestion(s) for extension

Children could go on to write an account of what happened in the village by the lake through the eyes of a villager, highlighting the feelings experienced at various points in the story.

Suggestion(s) for support

The groups should be mixed ability in order to combine very imaginative children with those who are less imaginative.

Assessment opportunities

The quality of discussion immediately following the story will indicate to what extent the children have identified with the imaginary world of the villagers. Listening to the group discussions and looking at the outcomes will provide evidence as to whether the children have understood that symbolism can be an expression of feelings and experience. At best, plans and designs will include imaginative detail which draws upon key elements of the story in creating symbols (see 'Key background information').

Opportunities for IT

The children can use a computer for several aspects of this work. They could use a word processor to:

▲ write what might happen at the weekly meeting;

▲ write accounts of what happened at the village;

The lake that turned to ice

The village lay beside a lake in the shadow of a large mountain. The villagers lived contented lives because the lake was unlike any other. As people in the village had done since the First Times, they had only to ask the lake for something and it would be given to them: food, baskets, mirrors, even living animals – anything they asked for.

But the villagers also knew (for it had been passed on since the First Times) that they had to obey three rules. First, they should never be greedy and ask for more than they needed. Second, though they were free to catch and eat all other fish in the lake, if a rainbow fish was caught it had to be returned to the lake at once. Third, each morning at sunrise, next to a great apple tree which grew by the water's edge, they must give something to the lake in return. So, at sunrise each day, golden apple juice from a large clay pot was poured into the lake.

One night, while the villagers lay asleep, two robbers crept into the village, and when they came to the water's edge, quietly asked the lake for gold coins, silver bars and precious gems. Feeling hungry, they then fished and, catching a rainbow fish in their net, cooked and ate it. Their bags and stomachs full, they crept away from the village as quietly as they had come.

At sunrise the following morning, a cry went up from the villagers who gathered at the apple tree to offer their daily gift. They found that the lake had turned into a huge block of ice. Nothing could be thrown or poured into it and, ask as they might, nothing came from the frozen surface.

The villagers were sad and knew that something had gone terribly wrong. Seeing the ashes of a fire and the remains of a rainbow fish, they realised that strangers had come and gone in the night. But, as they talked, they knew that they should feel grateful for all those years, since the First Times, when the lake had served the village so well.

So they decided that, even though the lake was no more, they needed to remember what it had done for them in the past. They agreed that each year, on the anniversary of the day when the lake had turned to ice, they would hold a festival in honour of the lake. They also decided to build a special building next to the apple tree where they could meet every week in order to remember and honour the lake. The building, they agreed, would be looked after by people who would wear special clothing and carry special objects during the weekly meeting and at the annual festival.

Though saddened by what had happened, the villagers once again grew contented with their lives in the shadow of the large mountain.

Display ideas

Under a heading such as 'The story of the lake that turned to ice', a map showing the location of the imaginary village could be displayed. A variety of other materials could also be displayed, including: plans and designs, models of the proposed building, ideas for special clothing in paper or fabric, drawings of symbols to decorate the building or clothing, suggestions for the annual festival and the weekly meeting, the story.

Reference to photocopiable sheet

Photocopiable page 157 gives the story of 'The lake that turned to ice' and is for the teacher's use at the beginning of the activity.

RELIGIOUS EDUCATION

SHORT GLOSSARY OF RELIGIOUS TERMS

For a full glossary of religious terms, consult the booklet *Religious Education – Glossary of Terms* published by the School Curriculum and Assessment Authority.

Adhan	The Muslim call to prayer.	**Gospel**	Literally 'good news'. The term 'Christian Gospel' refers to the central message of Christianity but when people refer to *the* Gospels they are referring to the four writings at the beginning of the New Testament.
Ahimsa	The doctrine of non-violence, respect for life, found in such religions as Buddhism, Hinduism and Jainism. Mahatma Gandhi extended this to achieving political ends through non-violent means.		
Allah	The Muslim word for God. Literally, it is Arabic for 'the God' (pronounced 'ull-lar').	**Granthi**	The Sikh, male or female, who reads from the Guru Granth Sahib (see below).
Arabesque	The symmetrical patterns distinctive of much art and design in Islam.	**Gurdwara**	A Sikh place of worship, literally the 'doorway to the Guru'.
Arti	A type of Hindu worship in which auspicious articles such as incense or light are offered to deities or saintly people.	**Guru**	The word means 'teacher'. In many religions, a guru is a spiritual teacher who gathers disciples. The Sikh religion began with Guru Nanak (1469–1539) after whom there were nine other Gurus. Today Sikhs regard their holy book as the Guru from whom they gain guidance and teaching.
Bar Mitzvah	A Jewish boy's coming of age at thirteen years. It is usually marked during synagogue worship and by a family celebration.		
Bat Mitzvah	A Jewish girl's coming of age at twelve years.	**Guru Granth Sahib**	The Sikh holy book which Sikhs believe to be their Guru (spiritual teacher). 'Granth' means 'book' while 'Sahib' is a term of honour.
Bible	The sacred book of Christians which is divided into the Old and New Testaments. It is, in reality, a library of books. The word 'bible' itself derives from the Greek word for 'books'.	**Hajj**	The Muslim pilgrimage to Makkah in Saudi Arabia made during the twelfth month of the year. One of the Five Pillars of Islam.
Bimah	The raised platform in a Jewish synagogue from which the Torah is read.	**Holi**	A Hindu festival occurring in the spring.
Buddha	A word that literally means 'Enlightened' or 'Awakened One' and applied by Buddhists particularly to Siddhartha Gautama after he received his enlightenment in the sixth century BCE.	**Huppah**	The canopy under which a bride and groom stand during the Jewish wedding ceremony (sometimes spelled 'chuppah').
Chanani	The canopy placed over the Sikh holy book as a mark of respect.	**Icon**	A devotional picture, usually painted on wood and showing Jesus, Mary or a saint, used by Orthodox Christians.
Chauri	The fan made of yak hairs or nylon which is waved over the Sikh holy book as a mark of respect.	**Id-Ul-Fitr**	The Muslim festival which celebrates the ending of Ramadan.
Christingle	A decorated orange used by some Christians to symbolise key beliefs during Christmas-time services.	**Ihram**	The white unsewn robes worn by male Muslims during their pilgrimage to Makkah.
		Islam	The title given to the religious way of life of Muslims. The Arabic word means 'submitted', a Muslim being a person who submits him/herself to the will of Allah.

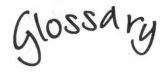

Glossary

Ka'bah	The cube-shaped building in the Holy Mosque in Makkah, Arabia, which is of great devotional significance to Muslims and towards which they face in prayer.
Kappel	Skull-cap worn by male Jews during religious activities and by Orthodox Jewish men all the time. Some Jews call it a 'kippah', others a 'yarmulke'.
Kaur	A Punjabi word meaning 'princess'. It is the name used by Sikh women.
Makkah	The birthplace of the Prophet Muhammad in Arabia and the focus of the Hajj or pilgrimage made by Muslims.
Mandir	A Hindu temple.
Manji	The large 'stool' on which the Sikh holy book is placed. Sikhs sometimes use the term 'manji sahib' as a mark of respect.
Mezuzah	The case containing a small scroll, affixed to the right doorposts of Jewish homes and buildings.
Mihrab	The mark or semi-circular recess in a mosque which indicates the direction of the Ka'bah in Makkah.
Minbar	The steps or raised platform in a mosque from which a talk is given during Friday midday prayers.
Mosque	The Muslim place of worship. The Arabic *masjid* literally means 'place of prostration'.
Mudra	The position of the hands and fingers of, for example, an image of the Buddha. A particular mudra will imply certain things.
Muezzin	In Islam, the person who makes the call to prayer (in Arabic, *Mu'adhin*).
Murti	A three-dimensional representation of a Hindu deity. The word 'idol' is avoided as it can cause offence.
Ner Tamid	The 'eternal light' found in a Jewish synagogue.
Parable	A story with a message and which often has an unexpected twist. Parables are particularly associated with the teaching of Jesus but many other teachers and religious figures have used them.
Pilgrimage	A journey to a place of religious or spiritual significance made for devotional reasons.
Prashad	A Hindu term referring to sacred or sanctified food.
Providence	The belief that God provides for his creation.
Qiblah	The 'direction' of the Ka'bah in Makkah which Muslims face during prayer/ worship five times daily.
Qur'an	The sacred book of Muslims. Its title derives from the Arabic word meaning 'to recite'. Muslims believe that the Qur'an consists of God's words which Muhammad was given over many years to recite. This spelling is now preferred to the older form 'Koran'.
Ramadan	The ninth month of the Muslim year during which Muslims fast during daylight hours.
Romallas	The decorative cloths which are used to cover the Sikh holy book.
Rosh Hashanah	Jewish New Year's Day.
Rupa	A term often used by Buddhists for an image of the Buddha. Literally 'form', 'body'.
Salah	Muslim prayer/worship, five times daily. One of the Five Pillars of Islam.
Sawm	Fasting during the daylight hours of Ramadan. One of the Five Pillars of Islam.
Sewa	A key Sikh teaching, meaning the service of others (pronounced 'say-va').
Shahadah	The Muslim declaration of faith, 'There is no God but Allah and Muhammad is the Messenger of Allah'. One of the Five Pillars of Islam.
Shema	The declaration of Jewish belief which begins, 'Hear, O Israel'. The title derives from the opening word: *shema* is Hebrew for 'hear' (pronounced 'sh'mah').

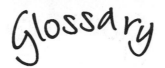
Glossary

SHORT GLOSSARY OF RELIGIOUS TERMS (continued)

Shirk	A term used in Islam for 'associating' something with Allah, which is absolutely forbidden.		Torah	The Hebrew word means 'instruction' or 'teaching' and is usually used by Jews as a title for the first five books of what Christians call the Bible.
Shofar	The curved ram's horn blown at some Jewish festivals.		Ummah	The community of Muslims, the 'nation of Islam'.
Singh	A Punjabi word meaning 'lion'. It is the name used by Sikh men.		Yad	A hand-held pointer used by a Jew when reading from the Torah (Hebrew 'hand').
Surah	A section or chapter of the Qur'an.			
Synagogue	A place of Jewish worship and education. The word literally means 'place of assembly'.		Yom Kippur	Jewish Day of Atonement, occurring on the tenth day after Rosh Hashanah.
Tallit	A fringed, four-cornered garment used by Jewish men during prayer in religious services. Often termed a 'prayer shawl'.		Zakah	The obligation to 'purify' your wealth by paying an annual welfare due. One of the Five Pillars of Islam.
Tawhid	Belief in the oneness of Allah, a central Muslim belief (pronounced 'Tore-heed').			

USEFUL BOOKS AND RESOURCES

Religious artefacts
The use of religious artefacts can greatly enliven teaching and learning in religious education. Though teachers will often find their own sources of religious artefacts, there are also several companies which publish catalogues so that artefacts may be ordered by post. Two examples are:
▲ *Articles of Faith*, Resource House, Kay Street, Bury, Lancashire BL9 6BU
▲ *Religion in Evidence*, Unit 7, Monk Road Industrial Estate, Alfreton, Derbyshire DE55 7RL

For background information about religious artefacts and ideas about how they might be used, the following book is indispensable: *Religious Artefacts in the Classroom* by Paul Gateshill and Jan Thompson (Hodder, 1992).

The following religious artefacts are included or alluded to in the activities in this book:
Buddhist
A statuette of the Buddha
Christian
Celtic cross
Latin cross
Palm cross
Crucifix
Hindu
Image or picture of Krishna
Jewish
Kippah (white)
Mezuzah case
Miniature Torah scroll
Yad
Shofar
New Year card
Tallit
Muslim
Plaque showing the shahadah
Prayer mat
Qiblah compass
Copy of the Qur'an
Ihram robes worn during Hajj
Sikh
Wedding garland (with portrait of Guru Nanak)

Sources of models
Card models of religious artefacts and buildings have sometimes been marketed. For example, Iqra Trust, a Muslim educational organisation, has produced card model kits of the Ka'bah and part of the Great Mosque in Makkah, the Dome of the Rock in Jerusalem, London Central Mosque and a Qur'an stand. For further information, contact:
▲ *Iqra Trust*, 24 Culross Street, London W1Y 3HE

Poster and picture packs
A number of major publishers, such as The Pictorial Charts Educational Trust, produce posters of relevance to religious education. For further information, contact:
▲ *PCET*, 27 Kirchen Road, London W13 0UD
The series of photographic packs produced by the Religious Education Centre in Birmingham is of particularly fine quality. The following packs are currently available:
▲ *Christians Photo Pack;*

Glossary

USEFUL BOOKS AND RESOURCES

▲ *Jews Photo Pack;*
▲ *Hindus Photo Pack;*
▲ *Muslims Photo Pack;*
▲ *Black Churches and Black Church Traditions Photo Pack.*
For further information, contact:
▲ *The Westhill RE Centre*, Westhill College, Selly Oak, Birmingham B29 6LL

Video programmes and packs
Many major publishers, such as the Religious and Moral Education Press (RMEP), include video material in their published list of resources. For further information, contact:
▲ *Religious and Moral Education Press*, St Mary's Work, St Mary's Plain, Norwich, Norfolk NR3 3BH

Video programmes are also included in the catalogue published by *Articles of Faith* (see 'Religious artefacts' on the previous page).

Some excellent video programmes are also available from organisations which have been established to provide educational resources about particular religious traditions. 'Buddhism for Key Stage 2', for example, is available from The Clear Vision Trust. For further information, contact:
▲ *The Clear Vision Trust*, 16–20 Turner Street, Manchester M4 1DZ

Recordings
Readings from the Qur'an and recordings of the Adhan, the Muslim call to prayer, are available from a number of Muslim organisations. For further information, contact *The Iqra Trust* (see 'Sources of models' on the previous page).

Subscription services for teachers of religious education
A number of organisations provide a regular supply of material and publications for teachers and others interested in religious education.

The Christian Education Movement (CEM)/Professional Council of Religious Education (PCfRE) offers a number of subscription services. Its termly mailing can include a number of periodicals such as the magazine *RE Today* (with an emphasis on practical classroom ideas) and the journals *British Journal of Religious Education* (with an emphasis on academic research), *Resource* (which contains articles of general interest), and *Look Hear!* (a review of recently published material relevant to religious education). The popular 'Teaching RE' series of booklets, with titles such as *Christmas*, *The Church*, *Buddhism* and *Festival* include those aimed at Key Stage 2. For further information, contact:
▲ *CEM*, Royal Buildings, Victoria Street, Derby DE1 1GW

Books about religion or religious themes
A large number of high-quality books about religions and religious themes are available. The following are recommended to support the activities in this book:
Creation Stories by Maurice Lynch (BFSS National RE Centre)

Creation Stories by Jon Mayled (Wayland, 1987).
Creation Stories: Anthology by Angela Wood (Educational Television Company Ltd, 1996).
Seasons of Splendour: Tales, Myths and Legends of India by Madhur Jaffrey (Puffin, 1995).
Teaching RE: Buddhism 5–11, edited by Pamela Wilkinson (CEM, 1995).

Reference books for children and teachers
Of the many excellent books which are now available, the 'Religions of the World' series (published by Simon & Schuster) is distinguished by the rich combination of very clear text with large, colour photographs and illustrations. The following titles are available:
The Buddhist World by Anne Bancroft;
The Christian World by Alan Brown;
The Hindu World by Patricia Bahree;
The Jewish World by Douglas Charing;
The Muslim World by Richard Tames;
The New Religious World by Anne Bancroft;
The Sikh World by Daljit Singh and Angela Smith.

For Bible stories, their background and ideas for further exploration, the following two books are outstanding:
Bible Stories for Classroom and Assembly: The Old Testament by Jack G. Priestley (RMEP, 1993).
Bible Stories for Classroom and Assembly: The New Testament by Jack G. Priestley (RMEP, 1994).

Background reading for teachers
Teachers will need to familiarise themselves with their locally agreed syllabus and any associated guidance material which has been produced. Other books of relevance to religious education are too numerous to mention. A list would include such books as:
Don't Just Do Something, Sit There – Developing Children's Spiritual Awareness by Mary Stone (RMEP, 1995).
Hindu Children in Britain by Robert Jackson and Eleanor Nesbitt (Trentham Books, 1992).
Religious Education and the Primary Curriculum by W. Owen Cole and Judith Evans-Lowndes (RMEP, 1994).
Teaching World Religions, edited by Clive Erricker (Heinemann Educational, 1993).

Other books and stories referred to in the text
Ask the Fellows who Cut the Hay by George Ewart Evans (Faber, 1975).
A Song for Every Season by Bob Copper (Paladin, 1975).
Bible Stories, retold by David Kossoff (Fontana, 1971).
Exploring Inner Space: Scientists and Religious Experience by David Hay (Penguin, 1982).
God-Talk with Young Children: Notes for Parents and Teachers by John M. Hull (CEM, 1990).
The Joys of Yiddish by Leo Rosten (Penguin, 1971).
Religious Experience Today: Studying the Facts by David Hay (Mowbray, 1990).

110

RELIGIOUS EDUCATION

Photocopiables

The pages in this section can be photocopied for use in the classroom or school which has purchased this book, and do not need to be declared in any return in respect of any photocopying licence.

They comprise a varied selection of both pupil and teacher resources, including pupil worksheets, resource material and record sheets to be completed by the teacher or children. Most of the photocopiable pages are related to individual activities in the book; the name of the activity is indicated at the top of the sheet, together with a page reference indicating where the lesson plan for that activity can be found.

Individual pages are discussed in detail within each lesson plan, accompanied by ideas for adaptation where appropriate – of course, each sheet can be adapted to suit your own needs and those of your class. Sheets can also be coloured, laminated, mounted on to card, enlarged and so on where appropriate.

Pupil worksheets and record sheets have spaces provided for children's names and for noting the date on which each sheet was used. This means that, if so required, they can be included easily within any pupil assessment portfolio.

Who do I admire most?, see page 14

A story about Guru Nanak

'Take this money, Nanak,' said Kalu. 'Go to town and buy goods. Then take them to market and sell them for a big profit.' Nanak took the coins that his father offered and set off, thinking to himself, 'I will make a good profit and make my father really proud of me.'

He had not gone far before he saw a group of holy men – the kind that you often see wandering on the roads in India – sitting by the side of the track. They looked tired and hungry and Nanak felt sorry for them. He asked them when they had last eaten and was surprised to hear that they had not eaten food for days.

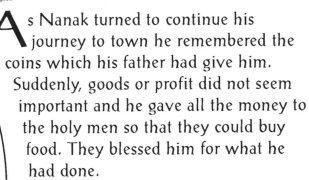

As Nanak turned to continue his journey to town he remembered the coins which his father had give him. Suddenly, goods or profit did not seem important and he gave all the money to the holy men so that they could buy food. They blessed him for what he had done.

Kalu was amazed to see his son Nanak return home so quickly. 'How much profit did you make!' he asked eagerly.

'I made no money,' Nanak replied, 'but I gained something far more important – blessings from a group of holy men.' Kalu was very angry when he realised what Nanak had done. This was not the kind of son that he had wanted.

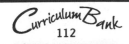
RELIGIOUS EDUCATION

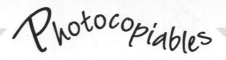
Who do I admire most?, see page 14

The person I admire most

Name _____   Date _____

▲ The name of the person I admire most is...

_____

▲ Some of the qualities of
this person that I admire are...

▲ This is my short story which shows
the qualities of this person.
(Continue on the back of this sheet if
you need to.)

▲ This is a picture of this
person or of something which
reminds me of this person.

**RELIGIOUS
EDUCATION**

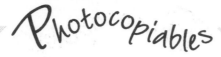

Will being rich make me a good person?, see page 17

The story of Malik Bhago and Lalo

Guru Nanak was on his travels again, visiting villages and towns and meeting many different kinds of people. Nearing one village, Nanak felt tired and hungry and he decided to spend a few days resting. A poor man called Lalo, who worked hard as a carpenter, invited Nanak to stay at his house and Nanak was happy to accept. When Malik Bhago, a rich and important man who lived in the same village, heard that the Guru was visiting the village, he sent his servants to invite Nanak to stay with him. 'I will give an enormous feast for all the important people in the area and Nanak, as my guest of honour, can sit by my side.'

Over a hundred people came to the feast, but Nanak was not among them. This made Malik Bhago very angry and he sent his servants to fetch Nanak. This time Nanak agreed to come. A crowd had gathered outside Malik Bhago's house, sensing that something was going on. Malik Bhago met Nanak at the door. 'Why did you refuse to come to my feast?' Malik Bhago asked. 'I had rich cake for you to eat but you preferred to eat coarse bread.'

Guru Nanak asked for a piece of the cake and took from his bag a piece of coarse bread which had been given to him at Lalo's house. He squeezed them both. To the surprise of the crowd, drops of milk trickled from the bread, while from the cake came drops of blood. Malik Bhago shouted, 'You are trying to trick me!'

But Guru Nanak answered, 'This is no trick. Lalo's simple bread was earned by honest work, but your fine cake, and all your wealth, was gained by cheating the poor.'

Malik Bhago thought about what Guru Nanak had said and he felt ashamed of the way that he had lived. From then on, he changed his ways and followed the teachings of Guru Nanak.

RELIGIOUS
EDUCATION

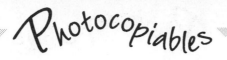

Statements

Name _____   Date _____

▲ Choose *five* statements which you believe to be important. There is space for you to add your own if you want to. Then put your five statements in order, from 1 (the most important) to 5.

People should be kind to animals.	Rubbish should be recycled.	People should believe in God.
Men and women should have the same opportunities.	People should live without taking illegal drugs.	Old people should be cared for by their families.
Drinking and driving is wrong.	People should take their litter home.	

What would I refuse to deny?, see page 19

The story of Bilal

Bilal held the whip high, but still the man called out, 'One God – there is only one God!' Slowly Bilal put the whip down. Even though he knew he would be punished, he could not beat this man. Bilal's master, Umaya, had ordered Bilal to beat the slave because he would not bow down and make offerings to the many statues and stones that surrounded the house. The slave talked to Bilal about his conviction that there was only one God and soon Bilal came to believe it too.

Umaya was furious. He was worried that all his slaves would turn against his ways, and the ways of his ancestors, and so he decided to punish Bilal and make an example of him. Bilal was taken into the desert outside the city of Makkah and made to lie in the full sun. But, even then, he called out, 'One God – there is only one God!'

Umaya was angrier than ever and called for a huge, heavy rock to be placed on Bilal's chest. Bilal found it difficult and painful to breathe with the heavy rock on his chest and his throat was dry and parched – but still he managed to murmur, 'One God – there is only one God!'

Many people passed by Bilal as he lay under the heavy rock. Only one tried to help. He was a man called Abu Bakr, a friend and companion of Prophet Muhammad. Abu Bakr went straight to Umaya and demanded that Bilal be released. But Umaya just laughed and said, 'I bought him. He belongs to me. I can kill him if I want to!' Abu Bakr knew the only way he could save Bilal's life was to buy him from Umaya, which he quickly did. He gave Bilal his freedom and soon he became a friend and companion of the Prophet Muhammad too. When, later, Muhammad and his friends left Makkah and went to the city of Madinah, far to the north, they met together to pray in the courtyard of Muhammad's house. But how would people know when it was time to stop what they were doing and gather together to pray! The solution was that someone could stand on the roof of Muhammad's house and, calling out in a loud voice, remind people that there is only one God and that it was time to gather for worship. But whose voice was loud enough and who was respected enough to be given this important job!

And so it was that Bilal became the first Muslim 'mu'adhin', the person who calls Muslims to prayer five times each day. Whereas once, as a man's slave, he had lain in the hot sand and only managed a whisper, he now stood proudly on the roof of Muhammad's house, a servant of Allah, and called out in loud but clear tones, 'God is most great! God is most great! There is only one God and Muhammad is the Prophet of God. Come to prayer. Come to prayer. God is most great!'

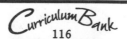

RELIGIOUS EDUCATION

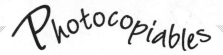

The story of Kisagotami

Kisagotami was the oldest daughter of the poorest man in the village. She was a frail, delicate girl, and her neighbours were certain that she would never find a husband. But her beautiful hair and shining eyes won the heart of a stranger, and Kisagotami left the village to join the family of her new husband. They treated her harshly because she was poor and tired easily, but all that changed when Kisagotami gave birth to the first son in her new family. Kisagotami's child was the joy of her life. Motherhood, too, brought respect and care from her relatives. Kisagotami had never known such happiness.

The boy grew strong and graceful. Then one day, at play in the forest, a snake bit him on the ankle. Within hours, Kisagotami and all her household were plunged into mourning. Her dearest was dead. Kisagotami was distraught with grief. She would not eat or sleep. She wandered, like a wild thing, round the houses of the villagers, cradling the body and pleading at every door for medicine to make her child well again. Her cries frightened the village. 'Whoever heard of medicine for the dead!' they muttered.

But Kisagotami's grief moved the heart of one person in the village. He was an old man, a follower of Gautama, the Buddha. He told her that Gautama was teaching in the next village. He might be able to give her medicine for her dead child.

That evening, Kisagotami started on her journey. All night she walked, carrying the child. She arrived at midday to find a large crowd gathered round Gautama. She pushed her way through and laid her child on the ground before him. A deep silence fell on the crowd.

'Exalted One,' she pleaded, 'give me medicine for my child.'

Gautama spoke to Kisagotami gently. 'Go to the city,' he told her. 'Visit every house. Bring me back a grain of mustard seed from every house that death has not visited. I shall wait for your return.'

Delight filled Kisagotami. At last, someone was listening. Here was one who would help. Through the city she wandered, knocking on every door, pleading for a grain of mustard seed if death had not entered there. She found herself listening to countless stories of sadness, the deaths of wives and husbands, of parents and children, of old age and sickness. In every house the story was different but the grief was the same, like Kisagotami's own grief. So Kisagotami learned compassion.

At length, she returned to seek Gautama. She found him waiting. She opened her empty hands. Neither spoke. Together they lifted the body of the child and carried him to the cremation grounds.

Adapted from a story by Maurice Lynch

The story of Kisagotami

Name _____   Date _____

1 Why did Kisagotami ask for medicine for her dead child?

2 Why didn't the Buddha simply tell Kisagotami that her son was dead?

3 How did Kisagotami eventually realise the truth?

4 Why is this a special story for Buddhists?

5 Has anyone in the group ever not wanted to accept the truth about something? Tell the group how you came to accept the truth.

RELIGIOUS
EDUCATION

When am I tempted?, see page 23

Temptations

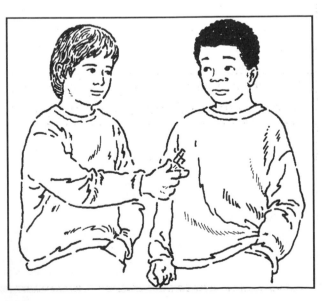

RELIGIOUS EDUCATION

Why did Jesus tell the story of the Good Samaritan?, see page 26

The parable of the Good Samaritan (1)

As he often did on his travels, Jesus sat in the shade of a tree speaking with a crowd of Jewish people. A man in the crowd, who everybody knew to be clever, suddenly asked Jesus, 'What must I do to live as God wants me to?'

'Well,' said Jesus, 'I think you already know the answer from what our holy writings say. They tell us that we must love God with all our hearts and love our neighbours as much as we love ourselves.'

The man thought about this for a moment and then asked, 'But who is my neighbour?'

Those people in the crowd who had heard Jesus answering questions like this before were not surprised to hear him start to tell a story.

'There was once a man who decided to travel alone along the road from Jerusalem to Jericho. He had just reached a very lonely spot when he heard a noise from behind the rocks at the side the road. As he looked up, robbers jumped out and attacked him. They knocked him on to the rocks, kicking and beating him. They ripped his clothes and stole everything that he was carrying. They left him bleeding and battered by the side of the road and in the full glare of the sun.

The man tried to get up but he was too badly hurt and couldn't even manage to crawl into the shade of the rocks.

After a little while, the sound of footsteps could be heard. It was a priest travelling up to the temple in Jerusalem where he had an important job to do, helping with the worship. The priest saw the battered traveller who looked as if he were dead.

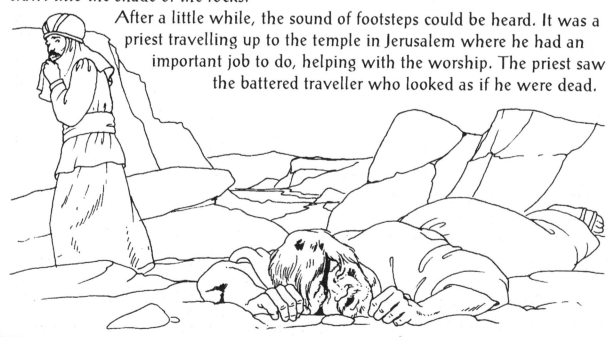

Why did Jesus tell the story of the Good Samaritan?, see page 26

The parable of the Good Samaritan (2)

Knowing that if he touched a dead body, he wouldn't be allowed to help with the worship, he walked by on the other side.

Some time later, another man walked down the road – a Levite, a person who helped the priests in the Jerusalem temple. He knew that robbers often used this part of the road to trick travellers. One of them would pretend to be hurt, and when someone stopped to help, the others would jump out and attack. Hardly glancing at the crumpled-up figure lying by the side of the road, the Levite quickly walked by on the other side.

Finally, someone came down the road who belonged to a group of people that the Jews really hated – the Samaritans. This Samaritan was riding on a donkey. He climbed off his animal and went over to the wounded traveller. Giving him a drink, he examined the wounds, putting ointment on the worst of them and bandaging them up. He then sat the stranger on his own donkey and,

leading the animal carefully, took him to the nearest inn. He asked the inn-keeper to look after the traveller and left some money to pay, saying that he would give more money if it was needed when he returned that way later.'

'So,' said Jesus, turning to the man who had asked the question, 'who do you think was the neighbour to the stranger!' Though the shortest answer would have been 'The Samaritan', the man's answer was, 'The one who was kind to him.'

'Well, then,' said Jesus, 'now you know what you have to do.'

RELIGIOUS EDUCATION

Do sisters and brothers ever understand each other?, see page 29

Sisters and brothers

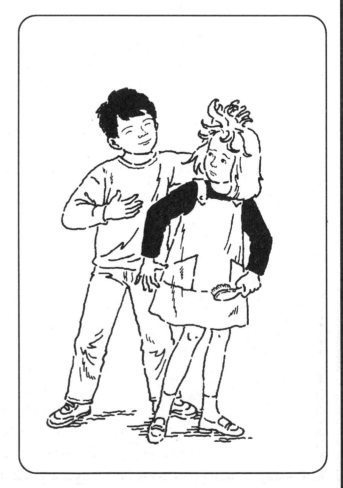

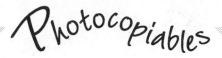
Why do people still love us when we're naughty?, see page 31

Krishna, the butter-thief

Yashoda loved her baby son, Krishna. Whenever she wasn't working in the house, she spent time with him. One day, Yashoda was making butter. Krishna loved to watch his mother stir the milk with a big stick and hear the glugging noise as it began to change into butter. After a while, Krishna felt hungry and wanted to be fed. He tugged at Yashoda's sari and she left her churning to feed her baby son. Then, suddenly, she remembered a pan of milk she had left to boil and went to remove it from the heat. Krishna was angry and upset that his mother had left so suddenly. He looked at the pot of freshly churned butter. Then he pushed the pot over and it cracked into pieces on the hard floor. He put his hands into the butter and licked his fingers. When Yashoda returned, she saw Krishna with butter around his mouth and on his fingers and she saw the broken pot with her freshly churned butter spilling on to the hard floor. Although Yashoda was angry with Krishna for spoiling her butter and for breaking the pot, she couldn't help smiling as she looked at her son covered in butter. She knew he must be punished, but she loved him even more.

RELIGIOUS EDUCATION

Should you help an enemy?, see page 32

The water-carrier

The battle had been raging for several weeks. The Sikh fortress was under siege and soldiers from both sides had been killed and badly wounded.

At the end of each day, one man made his way through the dying and wounded on the battlefield. He carried a bag of water on his back and, kneeling by the side of each wounded soldier, offered a drink as well as words of comfort.

A group of Sikh soldiers had been watching the man for days. They were angry that the man, a Sikh, was helping not only the Sikh wounded but their enemies as well. Finally, they could stand it no longer and decided to report him to the Guru.

'Bhai Ghanaya is helping our enemy. He should be punished!' they told the Guru. The Guru looked troubled and he sent for Bhai Ghanaya.

'I have heard that you are helping the enemy,' said the Guru. 'Is this true?'

'When I help the wounded,' replied the Sikh, 'I don't see friends or enemies. I only see injured people who are in need.'

The Guru was silent for a moment and then, turning to those who had complained, said, 'This man is a true Sikh!'

He turned back to Bhai Ghanaya and, giving him some ointment, told him to carry on doing his good work and to use the ointment to ease the pain of all wounded people on the battlefield.

RELIGIOUS EDUCATION

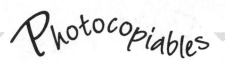

Why should we look after the Earth?, see page 39

Planet Earth

Name _____   Date _____

▲ You have heard the story *Dinosaurs and All That Rubbish.*
Write how each of the following characters felt in the story:

The man before he travelled in the rocket

The people who worked in the factories

The man after he had returned to Earth

The dinosaurs

RELIGIOUS EDUCATION

Why did Adam and Eve disobey?, see page 44

The story of Adam and Eve

Adam and Eve lived happily in the Garden of Eden. They looked after the plants and trees and ate their wonderful fruit. The snake watched them and was annoyed that they never ate from the tree in the middle of the garden.

One day, when Eve was alone, the snake quietly spoke to her, asking her why she never picked the fruit from the forbidden tree. 'God told us not to eat the fruit from that tree,' she replied. 'He said that we would die if we did.'

The snake sniggered. 'That's because he wants to keep that fruit for himself,' he said. 'He knows how special it is!'

'But why is it special?' asked Eve.

'If you eat that fruit, you'll know as much as God knows and you will be just like him,' the snake replied.

Eve looked at the tree in the middle of the garden. The fruit did look delicious and there was one piece just within her reach. 'Go on,' said the snake, 'take it. No one will ever know.'

Eve stretched out and picked the fruit and, before she knew what she was doing, she had taken a bite. The fruit was delicious and she ran to find Adam to let him taste it too. Adam took the fruit and bit into it.

Adam and Eve immediately realised that they were wearing no clothes and felt ashamed. They hid from each other until they had used fig leaves to cover themselves.

That evening, when they heard God walking in the garden, they hid from him. 'You have eaten from the forbidden tree,' God said to Adam. 'Why have you done such a thing?'

'Eve made me do it,' replied Adam.

'Don't blame me!' shouted Eve. 'It was the snake's fault.'

'From now on,' said God, 'you will not live in the Garden of Eden. You will go, and life will be hard for you. As a punishment, snakes will slither in the dust for ever.'

Adam and Eve left the Garden of Eden, never to return.

RELIGIOUS EDUCATION

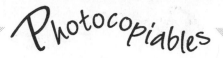

Questions on the story of Adam and Eve

Name _____   Date _____

1 Why do you think the snake waited until Eve was alone before it spoke to her?

5 How do you think God knew that they had eaten fruit from the forbidden tree?

2 Why do you think Eve took the fruit from the forbidden tree?

6 Why do you think Adam blamed Eve and Eve blamed the snake?

3 Why do you think Eve wanted Adam to eat the fruit?

7 Why do you think God sent them away from the Garden of Eden?

4 Why do you think they were ashamed after they had eaten the fruit?

8 Do you think there are any ways in which we are like Adam and Eve?

RELIGIOUS EDUCATION

What sights could make up stop and think?, see page 46

Life beyond the garden wall

Name _____   Date _____

Imagine that you have lived all your life in a large house surrounded by a huge garden. A large wall surrounds the garden and is so high that you cannot see over it. You have never been outside the wall.

Everything that you want is in the house, like good food, fine clothes and games to play. There are lots of young, healthy people to spend time with. There is, however, no way of finding out about what goes on in the world beyond the garden wall. There is no television or radio, and you never see newspapers.

You think that everyone in the world must live a life like yours. As you get older, though, you begin to wonder what life must be like beyond the wall. One day you climb over it.

▲ Think of at least four things that you might see in the world beyond the wall that would make you stop, think and be aware that life is not just about your own pleasure.

RELIGIOUS
EDUCATION

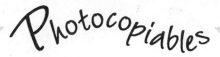
What sights could make us stop and think?, see page 46

The story of Siddharta Gautama's Four Sights (1)

Long ago, in the north of India, a baby son was born to a king and queen. They named him Siddhartha. There were celebrations throughout the land as news of the prince's birth spread. Many people came to give gifts to the new baby. Among them was a wise, old man who held the baby in his arms and said, 'This child will be great and will grow up to save the world from pain and suffering.'

The king was troubled at this for he wanted his son to be a great king like himself. The old man's words stayed in his head, so he decided to make sure that Siddhartha never saw pain or suffering. He wanted his son to concentrate on how to be a king. No one was allowed in the palace unless they were young and healthy, and Siddhartha was not allowed out beyond its great walls and gates.

So, Siddhartha grew up surrounded by beauty and happiness, knowing nothing of the outside world. In time, he married Yashodhara and they had a baby son. The king was happy. All was going to plan.

One day, Siddhartha was in the palace grounds with Chanda, his chariot-driver, when he saw the high wall which surrounded the palace. For the first time, he wondered what was on the other side of the wall. He went straight to his father to ask if he might be allowed to travel outside the gates and see his kingdom. The king knew that it would be impossible to prevent Siddhartha from going outside, so he sent out an order that only pleasant, happy sights were to be seen by his son.

The day came for Prince Siddhartha to leave the palace grounds. Riding with Chanda on a fine chariot, they were met by crowds of people scattering flower petals in front of them wherever they went.

They had not travelled far before Siddhartha caught a glimpse of a bent old man, slowly shuffling with the aid of a stick. 'What's the matter with that man?' Siddhartha asked Chanda.

RELIGIOUS
EDUCATION

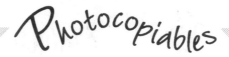

What sights could make us stop and think?, see page 46

The story of Siddhartha Gautama's Four Sights (2)

'He is an old man, your majesty,' replied Chanda. 'Old age comes to us all.' Siddhartha was puzzled by what he had seen and returned to the palace.

The next time he rode out, Siddhartha looked behind the rows of cheering people and saw a woman slumped in a doorway, her face and arms covered in sores. 'What's the matter with that woman?' Siddhartha asked Chanda.

'She is sick, your majesty,' Chanda replied.

'How did she become sick?' asked Siddhartha.

'People become sick for many reasons,' Chanda answered.

Once more Siddhartha returned to the palace.

Siddhartha left the palace a third time. Looking down a side-street he saw a line of people carrying a wrapped bundle on a stretcher. 'What's happening there?' he asked Chanda. 'What are those people doing?'

'That is a funeral procession, your majesty. That wrapped bundle is a dead person. Death comes to us all,' replied Chanda.

The prince was very troubled by this sight. Why should there be so much pain and suffering in the world? He returned to the palace.

On his fourth visit into the city, he saw a man dressed in simple clothes and carrying a bowl. 'Who is that, Chanda?' asked Siddhartha.

'Why, your majesty,' replied his charioteer, 'that is a holy man who has left all his possessions behind in order to wander the world in search of wisdom and truth. People help him by putting food into his bowl.'

Siddhartha returned to the palace deep in thought. All the riches which surrounded him had now lost their meaning. He was no longer contented. With Chanda's help, he made plans to leave the palace for ever.

One night, after looking at his sleeping wife and son for the last time, he made his way through the gate and went with Chanda to the outskirts of the city. There, he exchanged his fine clothes for a simple robe, gave his jewels to Chanda and cut off his long hair. He told Chanda to return to the palace and tell everyone that he would wander the world looking for the answer to pain and suffering.

Why did Jonah change his mind?, see page 52

Jonah and the fish

One day, God spoke to Jonah and said, 'Go to the city of Nineveh and tell everyone who lives there that I have seen how wicked they are and that I want them to live better lives.'

Jonah said, 'Yes God,' but he thought, 'I don't want to go to Nineveh where everyone is unkind. I will go somewhere else and God will never know.'

Jonah packed his belongings and went down to the harbour where he booked himself on a cargo boat bound for Spain. The little boat set sail on a calm sea, but it was not long before a great storm blew up around it. Lightning flashed, thunder crashed and huge waves threatened to fill the boat with water. The sailors were very frightened. They began to throw the cargo overboard to make the boat lighter but still it was in danger of sinking. The captain went to wake Jonah who was asleep below deck. 'Wake up, Jonah!' the captain shouted above the noise of the storm. 'Pray to your God for help so that we may be saved.'

'I cannot pray to God,' said Jonah. 'I am running away from him.'

The sailors realised that the storm had been sent by God to punish Jonah, who told them to throw him into the sea so that the storm would stop. But the sailors liked him and tried to get the boat back to shore. It was impossible. The storm was getting worse and worse. Knowing that they would all be drowned if they did nothing, the sailors now picked up Jonah and threw him into the sea. Immediately, the storm stopped and the water became calm again. The boat sailed on and Jonah was left alone, swimming far from the shore.

It wasn't long before Jonah felt a movement in the water beneath him and saw the shadow of a huge fish. The fish opened its mouth and sucked him inside, swallowing him in one gulp. Jonah found himself inside the stomach of the big fish. It was dark, wet and echoey. Jonah was very frightened and he prayed to God for help. He prayed for three days and three nights.

He had nearly given up hope when he felt himself being sucked out of the big fish's stomach, before being spat out on to soft, warm sand. As he stood up, he heard God's voice again telling him to go to Nineveh. This time Jonah set off at once to make the long journey across the desert to the foreign city.

RELIGIOUS
EDUCATION

What words could be used to guide a particular group of people?, see page 54

Living our lives

Name _____   Date _____

This is what our group thinks that people should do.

Children should try to...

Teachers should try to...

Parents should try to...

Everybody should try to...

People could be reminded of these words by:

RELIGIOUS
EDUCATION

The Bible

Name _____ Date _____

▲ Look up each of the references listed below in the Bible.
For each reference, read it, and then in your own words say how you think it might guide or help a Christian who was reading it.

The references are divided into three parts:
1   The title of the book in the Bible;
2   The chapter in the book;
3   The verses (each chapter is divided into these).
So, 'Psalm 1:1' means: The Book of Psalms + chapter 1 + verse 1.
The first two references below come from the first section of the Bible, the Old Testament. The second two come from the smaller second section, the New Testament. Some helpful information is given after each reference.

Reference	*How these words might help a Christian*
Exodus 20:12–13 These are two of the famous 'Ten Commandments'.	_____ _____ _____
Psalm 1:1 The psalms are songs of praise written by Jews long ago. The 23rd Psalm is probably the most well-known one.	_____ _____ _____
Luke 16:13 Luke, an early follower of Jesus, wrote about what Jesus did and what he thought it all meant.	_____ _____ _____
I Corinthians 13:13 This is part of a letter which Paul, a famous early Christian, wrote to the Christians in the Greek city of Corinth.	_____ _____ _____

RELIGIOUS EDUCATION

What are the Five Pillars of Islam?, see page 61

The Five Pillars of Islam (1)

Name _____   Date _____

RELIGIOUS EDUCATION

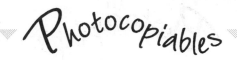

What are the Five Pillars of Islam?, see page 61

The Five Pillars of Islam (2)

Name _____   Date _____

1 How many pillars do Muslims try to act upon?	**6** What do Muslims do before they pray?
2 What is the Muslim word for God?	**7** In which direction do Muslims face when they pray?
3 Who do Muslims believe was the last Messenger of God?	**8** What is the word used for giving away some savings for good purposes?
4 How many times each day should Muslims pray?	**9** During which month do Muslims fast?
5 What language do Muslims use during this prayer?	**10** Where do Muslims go on pilgrimage?

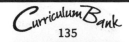
RELIGIOUS EDUCATION

How might the Five Precepts affect a Buddhist's life?, see page 63

A Buddhist's diary extract (1)

Name _____   Date _____

▲ Read the following extract from a young Buddhist's diary which shows how the person followed each one of the Five Precepts during the day. Underline those parts which you think show the person following a Precept. At the end, see if you can make a list of the Five Precepts that many Buddhists follow.

Today was a strange day and many things happened which made me think about being a Buddhist.

It wasn't the alarm clock that woke me up; it was a wasp buzzing loudly around my head. I got out of bed, rolled up a newspaper, let the wasp land on it and carefully carried it outside so that it could fly away.

I had promised to have lunch at Mary's house. On the way, I passed by a garden where some ripe strawberries were hanging over the wall. I love strawberries but managed not to pick any.

Mary had made a really good meal and – guess what? – there were strawberries for afterwards. She asked me if I wanted a second helping. I was tempted but said no.

After lunch we talked about school. Mary told me about an argument she had had with one of the teachers and began to tell me a story about something the teacher was supposed to have done. I quickly changed the subject and then left.

My friend came to visit in the evening. He had just got home from a holiday. He told me his brother had bought some lager on the ferry and had offered him a can. I said that I didn't think he ought to drink alcohol and that I wouldn't.

I went to bed and dreamed of strawberries!

The Five Buddhist Precepts
1
2
3
4
5

RELIGIOUS
EDUCATION

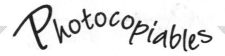

A Buddhist's diary extract (2)

Name _____   Date _____

▲ Read the following extract from a young Buddhist's diary which shows how the person followed each one of the Five Precepts during the day. Look at the list of Precepts at the bottom of the page and then underline the parts of the diary extract which you think show the person following each Precept.

Today was a strange day and many things happened which made me think about being a Buddhist.

It wasn't the alarm clock that woke me up; it was a wasp buzzing loudly around my head. I got out of bed, rolled up a newspaper, let the wasp land on it and carefully carried it outside so that it could fly away.

I had promised to have lunch at Mary's house. On the way, I passed by a garden where some ripe strawberries were hanging over the wall. I love strawberries but managed not to pick any.

Mary had made a really good meal and – guess what? – there were strawberries for afterwards. She asked me if I wanted a second helping. I was tempted but said no.

After lunch we talked about school. Mary told me about an argument she had had with one of the teachers and began to tell me a story about something the teacher was supposed to have done. I quickly changed the subject and then left.

My friend came to visit in the evening. He had just got home from a holiday. He told me his brother had bought some lager on the ferry and had offered him a can. I said that I didn't think he ought to drink alcohol and that I wouldn't.

I went to bed and dreamed of strawberries!

The Five Buddhist Precepts
1 Not to harm any living thing.
2 Not to take what is not freely given.
3 Not to be greedy.
4 Not to say unkind things.
5 Not to take drugs which cloud the mind.

How do Christians remember the events of Holy Week?, see page 66

Remembering the events of Holy Week

The days of Holy Week

Maundy Thursday	Easter Sunday
Palm Sunday	Good Friday

What happened

Jesus' tomb was found to be empty and some women followers met him again.	Jesus rode into Jerusalem on a donkey.
Jesus died on a cross and was buried in a stone tomb.	Jesus shared a last supper with his 12 special followers.

How Christians remember the events

Christians are sad and ornaments are covered up in some churches.	Christians are happy and churches are full of light.
In the UK, the King or Queen gives Maundy money to a group of old people.	Christians might be given crosses made from palm leaves.

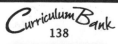
RELIGIOUS EDUCATION

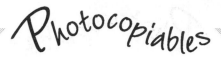

Why is light used as a symbol at Christmas?, see page 68

Christingle

Name _____ Date _____

▲ Name the parts of the Christingle and explain what they symbolise.

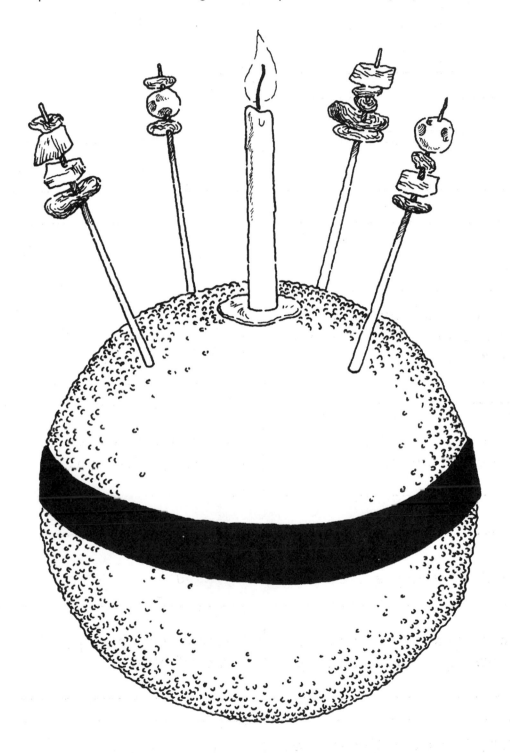

▲ Christians believe that Jesus brings light to the world. What do you think they mean by this? (Write on the back of this sheet.)

RELIGIOUS EDUCATION

Photocopiables

Why is light used as a symbol at Christmas?, see page 68

The Festival of Saint Lucia

▲ Read about what happens in Sweden on Saint Lucia's Day each year.
What *symbols* are included and what do you think they mean?

Each year in Sweden, on 13 December, the festival of Saint Lucia takes place.
In many parts of Sweden, girls dress up as Saint Lucia. They wear long white dresses with red sashes around their waists. Each girl wears a crown made from evergreen leaves and lighted candles. A number of other girls accompany the one dressed as Saint Lucia. They also wear white dresses with red belts, but their crowns are made of tinsel. They each carry a lighted candle.
Sometimes, first thing on 13 December, parents are woken up by their eldest daughter who has dressed up as Saint Lucia. She might sing them a song before giving her parents coffee and special Saint Lucia biscuits and cakes.

RELIGIOUS
EDUCATION

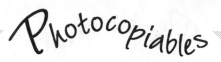

What happened on the first Easter Sunday morning?, see page 70

The first Easter Sunday morning

Name _____   Date _____

Four early Christians – Matthew, Mark, Luke and John – each wrote an account of what happened when, at first light on the Sunday morning, people went to the tomb in which Jesus' body had been placed. Look at each of these accounts in turn and, using the questions below as a guide, write a summary of what each writer wrote. If you have time, compare the four summaries, looking for similarities and differences.

	Mark, chapter 16, verses 1–8	Matthew, chapter 28, verses 1–10	Luke, chapter 24, verses 1–11	John, chapter 20, verses 1–18
◀ Who went to the tomb?				
◀ When did they go?				
◀ Why did they go?				
◀ What were they thinking about?				
◀ What did they see and hear at the tomb?				
◀ What did they do?				

RELIGIOUS EDUCATION

What are the origins of the familiar Christmas story?, see page 73

Where the Christmas story began

Name _____   Date _____

▲ Two early Christians – Matthew and Luke – wrote about what happened when Jesus was born. Some details were only included by Matthew and some only by Luke. Sometimes both Matthew and Luke included the same details.

Read Matthew's account (chapter 2, verses 1–15) and then Luke's account (chapter 2, verses 1–20). Then, using the columns below, note down the details which:
1 only Matthew includes;
2 only Luke includes;
3 both of them include.

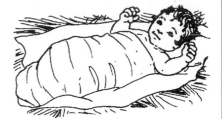

Only included in Matthew	Only included in Luke	Included in both Matthew and Luke

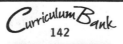
RELIGIOUS EDUCATION

When do Jewish children become adult?, see page 75

What happens at a Jewish Bar/Bat Mitzvah?

Name _____   Date _____

RELIGIOUS
EDUCATION

What do Jews do at Rosh Hashanah and Yom Kippur?, see page 77

Rosh Hashanah and Yom Kippur

Name _____ Date _____

▲ Referring to the list at the bottom of this sheet, fill in the missing words.
When you complete sentences, think carefully about the reasons you are giving.

1 Rosh Hashanah is the Jewish _____ Year.

2 Some Jews eat pieces of apple dipped in _____ to show...

3 In the _____ days between Rosh Hashanah and Yom Kippur,
Jews ask for _____ from those to whom they might have done
wrong over the last year.

4 Yom Kippur is the most _____ day of the Jewish year.

5 On Yom Kippur, Jews go to the _____ to ask forgiveness of
_____.

6 Many Jews wear _____ on Yom Kippur to show...

7 Jews fast on Yom Kippur because...

8 At the end of Yom Kippur, a ram's horn called a _____ is blown
in the synagogue.

solemn	white	forgiveness	shofar	New
synagogue	God		ten	honey

RELIGIOUS EDUCATION

How can a church reveal what Christians think is important?, see page 81

Thinking about a church building

Name _____ Date _____

▲ What did you see or hear during your visit to the church building which shows that each of the following ten things are important to Christians?

Believing in God?
Following Jesus?
Reading and knowing the Bible?
Worshipping and praying together?
Making the church a special place?
Teaching and learning about being a Christian?
Welcoming people into the Christian community?
Helping others?
Telling others about being a Christian?
Remembering people?

Why is the synagogue special for Jews?, see page 83

The Jewish synagogue

Name _____   Date _____

▲ Read the following passage and fill in the missing words using the list below it.
Be careful: some words are used more than once.

At the front of a _____, there is a special cupboard called an

_____. It has _____ hanging in front of it and a _____

hanging above it. Torah _____ are kept inside it to keep them safe.

_____ sit facing the _____ and watch carefully as the

_____ are taken out to be read aloud during _____.

| lamp | worship | synagogue | curtains | ark | Jews | scrolls |

▲ Write about what makes the synagogue a special place for Jews.

▲ Draw the Torah scrolls inside the ark.

**RELIGIOUS
EDUCATION**

Why is a mosque built as it is?, see page 85

A simplified ground plan of a mosque

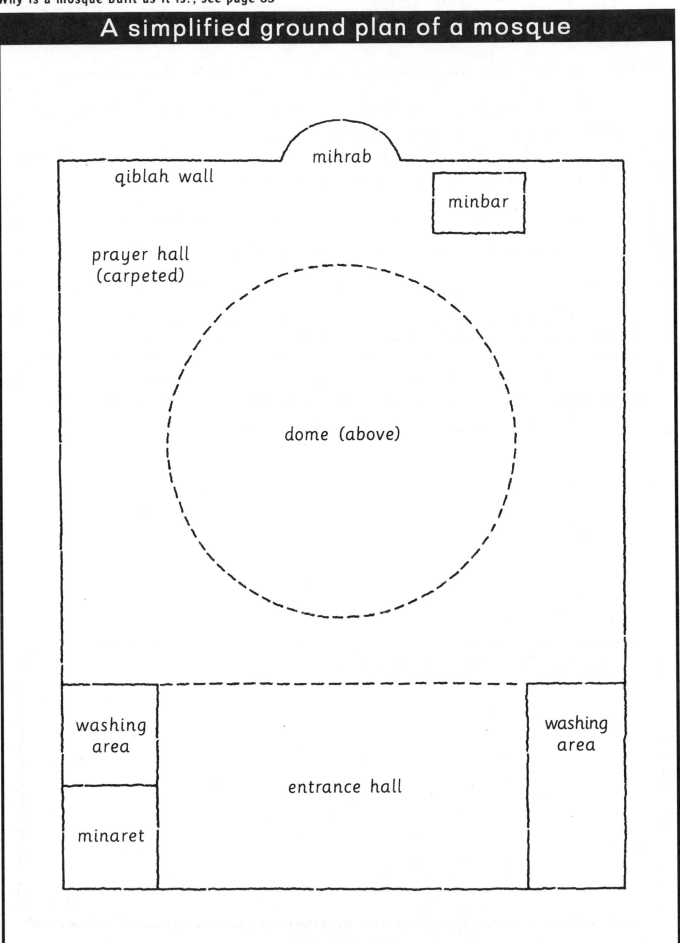

mihrab

qiblah wall

minbar

prayer hall
(carpeted)

dome (above)

washing
area

washing
area

entrance hall

minaret

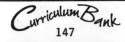

Photocopiables

Why is a mosque built as it is?, see page 85

The features of a Muslim mosque

This shows that the prayer hall and the mosque are special.		A dome	A room where there is fresh running water
	A raised platform	The minaret	The call to prayer is called out from this.
The largest area in the mosque in which the floor is covered with a carpet	A tall tower with a balcony		The washing area
	The place where Muslims can prepare themselves for prayer by washing	The wall at the front of the prayer hall	The minbar
This is over the prayer hall and might be painted gold outside.	The qiblah wall	Muslims gather in here to pray after they have taken off their shoes.	The prayer hall
A Muslim stands on this to give a talk during special prayers on Friday.		This shows that the whole room faces in the direction of Makkah.	

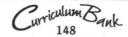

RELIGIOUS EDUCATION

Why is the Ka'bah a special place for Muslims?', see page 88

The Ka'bah – A special place for Muslims

The Ka'bah is a cube-shaped building which stands in the large courtyard of the Great Mosque in Makkah, Saudi Arabia. Only Muslims are allowed to visit Makkah. There is only an empty room inside the Ka'bah: it is the spot which it marks which is important. The Ka'bah is made of stone blocks but is covered with a heavy black cloth which has words from the Holy Qur'an embroidered on it. In one corner of the Ka'bah is the famous Black Stone, which Muslims believe is the oldest part of the Ka'bah.

Each year at a certain time, millions of Muslims make a pilgrimage to Makkah. Rich or poor, they all wear simple white clothes. Even though there will be huge crowds and they will be hot and tired, it will be an experience that pilgrims never forget. The pilgrimage begins with a visit to the Great Mosque. Pilgrims enter the mosque and then walk or jog seven times around the Ka'bah saying prayers in Arabic. This is called 'greeting' the Ka'bah. The lucky ones touch the Black Stone but others raise a hand towards it as they pass it by. In the courtyard near the Ka'bah is a well called Zam Zam. Pilgrims go to this and drink some water from it. Many will take some water home with them so that, when they return, friends and family who could not go will be able to share some of the excitement with them.

▲ Choose *one* of the following tasks. In your account, try to include feelings as well as information.

1 Imagine that you are a British Muslim. You are on pilgrimage to Makkah. Write a diary account of your first day in Makkah when you visit the Ka'bah and see it for the first time.

2 You work for a Muslim newspaper in Glasgow, Scotland. You are on pilgrimage to Makkah but have been asked to write a newspaper article about what you experience. Write a short article about what you saw when you visited the Ka'bah for the first time.

RELIGIOUS
EDUCATION

What might you experience in a Hindu mandir?, see page 91

A first visit to a Hindu temple (1)

It was the first time that I had visited a Hindu temple and I was feeling a little uncertain as I walked in through the door. The first thing that I noticed was that people were taking off their shoes and putting them on racks. I took off my shoes and put them at the end where I would be able to find them again. There were sinks by another door. As people passed by, they quickly rinsed their hands and dried them on a towel. I was too embarrassed to do this and simply followed some other people through the doorway.

I found myself in a large room with carpet on the floor and the air filled with a smell which was heavy and sweet. I saw that there were many pictures on the walls and also some writing, some of it in English but some in a language I couldn't read. At the front, where most of the people were standing, I could see bright lights and colours. As I got nearer, I saw several statues of men and women dressed in fine clothes with strings of flowers around their necks. They were standing on a raised platform which had a top to it. It was decorated with coloured lights and tinsel. Around the feet of the statues were smaller statues of animals like an elephant and a monkey. Near to the animals were bottles of milk, flowers and even some coconuts. A man in white was holding a dish with lighted candles which he was waving around in front of the faces of the statues. Everyone was singing and one lady was ringing a large bell which was hanging down from the ceiling on a chain.

When everyone stopped singing and the lady stopped ringing the bell, the man dressed in white took the dish with the lighted candles to each person. Many of them put money in it, and then put their hands over the flame and wiped the sides of their face and hair with their hands. When everyone had had a turn, the man in white brought the candle to me, but I shook my head. The man smiled at me and went away.

People started to leave, and I went to the front to have a closer look at the statues. I now saw where the smell was coming from. On the platform near the statues were bundles of thin sticks which were smoking.

I headed towards the door, and a lady pushed a small bag into my hand and gave me a big green apple. I found my shoes on the rack outside and quickly put them on. As I walked out into the street, I looked inside the bag to see nuts and other good things to eat. I took a bite out of my apple and began to think about what I had just seen.

RELIGIOUS
EDUCATION

A first visit to a Hindu temple (2)

Name _____   Date _____

1 Why do you think the person went to the Hindu temple?

6 Why were the statues so finely dressed?

2 Why did the Hindus take off their shoes and wash their hands?

7 Who do you think the man in white was?

3 Should the person have washed her hands?

8 Why do you think the lady was ringing the bell?

4 What was the big room with the carpet?

9 Why do you think the girl didn't want to put her hands over the candles?

5 Who do you think were shown in the pictures on the walls?

10 Why do you think the lady gave the girl an apple and a bag of food?

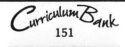
RELIGIOUS
EDUCATION

What beliefs are represented in a Christian graveyard?, see page 94

A Christian graveyard

Name _____   Date _____

Remember to walk quietly and think about where you are.

▲ Find three examples of words on gravestones which show that Christians believe that death is not the end. Write them here.

▲ Find two examples of pictures on gravestones. What are the pictures of? Why have they been put there?

▲ Find two examples of carvings as part of or next to a gravestone. Draw them. Why have Christians put them there?

▲ Find three different kinds of plants/trees/flowers which have been planted or put in the graveyard. Draw them. Why are they there?

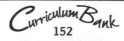
RELIGIOUS EDUCATION

How do people express themselves through patterns?, see page 96

Muslim calligraphy and Arabesque

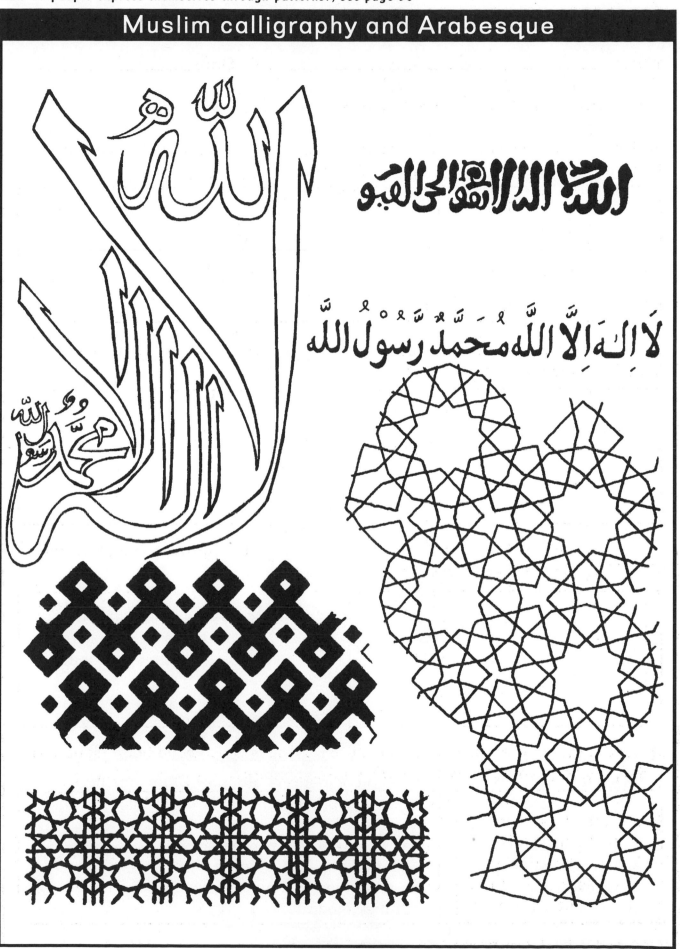

Why are there different kinds of cross?, see page 100

Different types of Christian cross

Name _____   Date _____

▲ Below are six types of Christian cross. Draw a line to match the descriptions to the drawings.

The Latin Cross

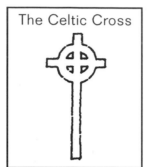

The Celtic Cross

The Greek Cross

St Andrew's Cross

Russian Orthodox Cross

Maltese Cross

▲ This cross has four arms of equal length.

▲ This eight-pointed cross has been used by the St John's Ambulance Brigade.

▲ This is probably the most common shape of cross seen in the Western world.

▲ The top line probably represents the sign that was put over Jesus' head, and the bottom line the ledge on which Jesus' feet rested.

▲ Many examples of this cross can be found in Wales, Scotland and Ireland.

▲ This cross is named after one of the close followers of Jesus who, it is said, was tied to an X-shaped cross.

Imagine that you work for a design company. A group of Christians has asked you to design a new cross to represent the following ideas:
1   that Christianity is worldwide;
2   that Christianity encourages care for the environment;
3   that Christianity is for people of all ages.
▲ Choose *one* of these ideas, design a cross to represent it and then label the various parts to show what they mean.

Why do people pray differently?, see page 102

Positions that people adopt for prayer

1

2

3

4

5

6

RELIGIOUS
EDUCATION

What do Hindus learn from the story of Krishna's birth?, see page 103

The birth of Krishna

There was once a wicked king called Kans who ruled over a kingdom in India. Devaki, his younger sister, was getting married to Vasudev. Just as the wedding celebrations were coming to an end, Kans heard a voice saying that a baby born to Devaki and Vasudev would eventually kill him. Kans was angry, and threw his sister and her new husband into prison. After a while, Kans heard from the prison guards that Devaki had had a baby daughter. Kans ordered the baby to be killed. As the prison guards tried to kill the baby girl, she turned and said, 'I am not the baby you are looking for. Another yet to be born will kill the king.'

Six other children were born, and the king ordered each one to be killed, but each one said the same thing.

The eighth baby to be born was a boy whom Devaki called Krishna. No sooner had he been born than Vasudev heard a voice telling him to take his baby son across the river to his sister Yashoda's house and exchange him for her new-born baby girl. Vasudev wrapped up baby Krishna and placed him in a basket. To his amazement, he found the cell doors were unlocked and that all the prison guards were in a deep sleep. Vasudev carried baby Krishna to the banks of the river which was deep and fast-flowing. Vasudev lifted the baby in the basket above his head to keep him dry and safe. He waded into the river and the waters rose higher and higher. Soon they were lapping around Vasudev's chin, who thought that they would both drown. Baby Krishna gently lowered his foot over the side of the basket until it touched the foaming waters. At once, the river became still and parted to allow father and son to walk safely across to the other side. As soon as they had crossed, the waters closed behind them.

Vasudev went straight to Yashoda's house and told her what had happened. They swapped Krishna for Yashoda's new-born baby girl and, leaving Krishna with Yashoda, Vasudev returned with the baby girl to the prison cell.

Next morning, when the king heard that Devaki had had another baby, he again sent for the baby to be killed. But before the guards could kill the baby, she shouted, 'Krishna is born already and is safe far away!' When Kans heard that he had been tricked, he was very angry and he gave an order that all baby boys in his kingdom under the age of 12 months were to be killed. He did not know that Krishna was safe because he was across the river in another kingdom.

RELIGIOUS EDUCATION

The lake that turned to ice

The village lay beside a lake in the shadow of a large mountain. The villagers lived contented lives because the lake was unlike any other. As people in the village had done since the First Times, they had only to ask the lake for something and it would be given to them: food, baskets, mirrors, even living animals – anything they asked for.

But the villagers also knew (for it had been passed on since the First Times) that they had to obey three rules. First, they should never be greedy and ask for more than they needed. Second, though they were free to catch and eat all other fish in the lake, if a rainbow fish was caught it had to be returned to the lake at once. Third, each morning at sunrise, next to a great apple tree which grew by the water's edge, they must give something to the lake in return. So, at sunrise each day, golden apple juice from a large clay pot was poured into the lake.

One night, while the villagers lay asleep, two robbers crept into the village, and when they came to the water's edge, quietly asked the lake for gold coins, silver bars and precious gems. Feeling hungry, they then fished and, catching a rainbow fish in their net, cooked and ate it. Their bags and stomachs full, they crept away from the village as quietly as they had come.

At sunrise the following morning, a cry went up from the villagers who gathered at the apple tree to offer their daily gift. They found that the lake had turned into a huge block of ice. Nothing could be thrown or poured into it and, ask as they might, nothing came from the frozen surface.

The villagers were sad and knew that something had gone terribly wrong. Seeing the ashes of a fire and the remains of a rainbow fish, they realised that strangers had come and gone in the night. But, as they talked, they knew that they should feel grateful for all those years, since the First Times, when the lake had served the village so well.

So they decided that, even though the lake was no more, they needed to remember what it had done for them in the past. They agreed that each year, on the anniversary of the day when the lake had turned to ice, they would hold a festival in honour of the lake. They also decided to build a special building next to the apple tree where they could meet every week in order to remember and honour the lake. The building, they agreed, would be looked after by people who would wear special clothing and carry special objects during the weekly meeting and at the annual festival.

Though saddened by what had happened, the villagers once again grew contented with their lives in the shadow of the large mountain.

RELIGIOUS
EDUCATION

INFORMATION TECHNOLOGY WITHIN RELIGIOUS EDUCATION

Main IT focus

The information technology activities outlined in this book can be used to develop and assess children's IT capability as outlined in the National Curriculum. The main emphasis for the development of IT capability within these activities is on communicating information.

Word processing

Many of the activities and extension ideas in this book which incorporate some form of writing activity can be used to develop children's IT capability through the use of a word processor.

During Key Stage 2, children should be developing their confidence and competence to use word-processing or desktop publishing packages. Many word processors now have basic desktop publishing features and it may be possible to use a single piece of software for most writing tasks.

A key difference, however, between the two types of software is the way in which text is placed on the page. In a desktop publishing package text is generally placed inside a frame which can be altered in size and shape; the text is automatically reformatted to fill the new shape. This provides a flexible way for children to organise text and pictures on a page and to experiment with different types of page design.

Children should already have a basic knowledge of the keyboard and should be given opportunities to develop some of the more sophisticated aspects of using a word processor or desktop publishing package. These should include learning how to:

▲ use more than a single finger/hand when typing, particularly as they become more proficient and know where letters are located;
▲ separate and join text using the return and delete keys;
▲ move the cursor to a mistake and correct it without deleting all the text back to the mistake;
▲ scroll around the document using the mouse or cursor keys;
▲ select an appropriate font from a menu;
▲ change the size and/or colour of a font;
▲ underline a word or line;
▲ alter the style of a word or sentence, for example using italics or bold;
▲ centre the text using the centre command;
▲ use the tab key to create columns;
▲ justify text so that it lines up against the right hand margin, and reset this option;
▲ save and retrieve their work from the disk, eventually unaided;
▲ print their completed work unaided;
▲ use a spelling checker to check their work;
▲ add a picture to their work, positioning and re-sizing it.
Higher order skills might include:
▲ altering the ruler to change margins and set tab keys;
▲ adding page numbers;
▲ adding a table;
▲ setting up a master page to create a consistent layer throughout a document;
▲ setting up a text style to use within the document.

It is important for teachers or other adults to be available to intervene as children are working in order to teach them new skills appropriate to the task being undertaken. Children should also be given opportunities to originate their work at the computer keyboard rather than always writing it out longhand and simply using the word processor to make a 'fair copy' for their folder or display purposes. It is often appropriate for children to make their first draft at the keyboard, save it, print it out and then redraft it away from the keyboard, thus giving another child the opportunity to use the computer.

Some of the activities suggest the use of word-processed files created in advance by the teacher for the children. Such activities reduce the necessity for text entry and can enable children to concentrate on the concept being studied or on the more sophisticated word-processing commands of editing, organising and presenting work for an audience. When such files are created, ensure that a backup is kept and where possible the 'master' file is locked against accidental overwriting.

CD-ROMs

Many of the activities in this book could be extended through the use of CD-ROMs for children to research other information about the area being studied.

The most useful types of CD-ROM for this work are those which provide an encyclopaedia type of environment, either as an encyclopaedia or as a resource on a single theme. These CD-ROMs contain text and pictures, with some of the more recent ones including moving pictures, music, sound effects and speech. Children can access the information in a number of ways. If they wish to make a simple search for the topic in which they are interested, such as Sikhism, they can type in the word 'gurdwara', for example. This will then take them to the relevant part of the CD-ROM. When they read the page they may also find that some of the words are highlighted in a different colour. By clicking on these words they will be taken to another section of the encyclopaedia which has more, or linked, information. Moving from one part to another via these 'hot links' is called browsing.

A good starting point for children is for the teacher to set some information to be found using the CD-ROM. This ensures that the information is available for the children. Once this has been found the children can explore other parts of the CD-ROM for further information.

IT links

The grids on this page relate the activities in this book to specific areas of IT and to relevant software resources. Types of software rather than names of specific programs have been listed to enable teachers to use the ideas regardless of the computers to which they have access. The software featured should be available from most good educational software retailers. Teachers may still want to include specific software which runs on their computers and which addresses the content and understanding of the religious education being taught. Activities are referenced by page number rather than by name (bold page numbers indicate activities which have expanded IT content).

AREA OF IT	SOFTWARE	ACTIVITIES (PAGE NOS.)						
		CHAP 1	CHAP 2	CHAP 3	CHAP 4	CHAP 5	CHAP 6	CHAP 7
Communicating Information	Word processor	15, **17**, 19, 20	32, 35	43, 48	54, 57	70	81, 85	**98**, 105
Communicating Information	DTP	15, **17**	35		52	70		
Communicating Information	Drawing package		34	38, 41, 48	54	68	89	100, 105
Communicating Information	Art package		28, 34	38, 41, 48	57			100, 105
Communicating Information	Framework						81, 85	
Communicating Information	Multimedia		**35**		52		**91**	
Information Handling	CD-ROM	14, 19		46	54, 61	70, 75	83, 85, 88, 89	
Information Handling	Database				57			
Software	Graphing software	21						

SOFTWARE TYPE	BBC/MASTER	RISCOS	NIMBUS/186	WINDOWS	MACINTOSH
Word processor	Folio Pendown	Pendown 2 Desk Top Folio	All Write Write On	Word Kid Works 2 Creative Writer	Kid Works 2 EasyWorks Creative Writer
DTP	Front Page Extra Typesetter	Desk Top Folio 1st Page Pendown DTP	Front Page Extra NewSPAper	Creative Writer NewSPAper	Creative Writer
Framework		My World 2		My World 2	
Art package		1st Paint Kid Pix Splash		Colour Magic Kid Pix 2	Kid Pix 2
Drawing Software		Draw Vector Art Works		ClarisWorks Oak Draw	ClarisWorks
Multimedia Authoring		Magpie Hyperstudio Genesis		Genesis Hyperstudio Illuminus	Hyperstudio Hyperslider
Database	Grass	Junior Pinpoint Find IT KeyNote	Grass	Sparks ClarisWorks Information Workshop	ClarisWorks EasyWorks
CD-ROM		Children's Micropaedia Hutchinsons		Encarta 96 Children's Micropaedia Grolier	Encarta 96 Grolier
RE CD-ROM		Aspects of Religion		Aspects of Religion New family Bible Sources of faith	Sources of Faith

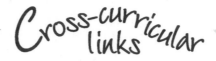

Cross-curricular links

	ENGLISH	MATHS	SCIENCE	HISTORY	GEOGRAPHY	D&T	ART	MUSIC
LIVING WITH OURSELVES	Discussing artefacts. Writing a newspaper article. Writing a play script. Writing a diary extract. Using role-play.	Carrying out a whole school survey to ascertain responses.		Dating the beginning of the Sikh religion.			Drawing a picture of a person who is most admired.	
LIVING WITH OTHERS	Dramatising a biblical story. Using a range of descriptive words. Writing and reading stories. Listening to stories from a range of cultures.		Thinking about the life-giving properties of water.	Thinking about events in their own lives. Writing about one event from differing points of view.	Using a 'key' to explain a plan.		Using fabric to represent ideas, memories and experiences.	
LIVING IN THE WORLD	Writing and reading stories. Listening to stories from a range of cultures. Writing poems and newspaper accounts.		Discussing ideas and theories about how the world began. Thinking about ecological balance, about growth and death.	Identifying different viewpoints. Learning about the importance of harvest in the past.	Thinking about how people's actions affect the environment. Thinking about how concern for living things could be promoted.		Using paint to express ideas and feelings. Using pattern and texture in bark and leaf rubbings. Responding to the work of artists.	Listening to atmospheric music. Looking at harvest hymns.
FOLLOWING GUIDANCE	Discussing artefacts. Looking at different scripts. Dramatising part of a biblical story.					Designing and making a special container.	Creating a decorative script.	
ENCOUNTERING SPECIAL TIMES	Discussing artefacts. Listening to stories from other cultures.			Using source material to establish similarities and differences.				
ENCOUNTERING SPECIAL PLACES	Listening to stories from different cultures. Writing stories and poems.				Investigating a church close to the school environment. Direction-finding. Using a special compass to find Makkah.	Designing a room in which to house a special book.	Expressing ideas and feelings through painting pictures.	Listening to evocative music. Composing music to express feelings.
EXPRESSING WHAT IS IMPORTANT	Discussing artefacts. Discussing the role of story.	Investigating pattern and shape.		Using graveyards as a source for learning about the past. Remembering wars.	Investigating the locality of the school. Making a map of an imaginary village.	Designing a cross to communicate ideas and messages.	Looking at art and design from different cultures. Investigating how images and pictures in graveyards communicate ideas. Using pattern to communicate ideas.	